FEAR TO LOVE

AN INNER JOURNEY HOME

By

Belinda Bennetts

FEAR TO LOVE

AN INNER JOURNEY HOME

Copyright © Belinda Bennetts 2015

ISBN – 13: 978 – 1522707905

ISBN – 10: 1522707905

All rights reserved

No part of this book may be reproduced in any form, by photocopying or by any electronic means, including information storage or retrieval systems, without permission in writing from both the copyright owner and the publisher of this book.

This book is a work of non-fiction.

The author asserts her moral rights.

Contents

Dedication
Introduction
Part One: Self Inquiry
1   Who am I?
2   Fear
3   Anger
4   Guilt
Part Two: Surrender
5   The early years
6   The little Church on the farm
7   Gift or Curse?
8   Springvale
9   Memories of England
10   The Happy Years
11   The Winds of Change
12   The People of Africa
13   Darker Days
14   My Father's Death
15   Alcoholism
16   Granny's Death
17   Dance of the Heart then back to School
18   Rose Tinted Glasses
19   The End of an Era
20   Across the World
21   Stepping into the New
22   Studies and a New Path
23   Reconnecting
24   The Plains of Emptiness

25	Pregnancy
26	Motherhood
27	And then there was Chaos

Part Three: Coming Home

28	Core Beliefs
29	The Doors of Perception
30	Purpose and Love
31	The Three Steps are Revealed
32	A Deeper Remembering
33	Parting Words

Acknowledgements
About Belinda Bennetts

Dedication

My daughter Lucy Rose: I am so very proud of all that you are.

My sister Victoria: for being there, for being you.

My mother: you taught me so much, I love you

To Ellen: your kindness and friendship I will cherish forever

To Kim: our paths were meant to cross, thank you

To my readers: may you follow your passion, follow your dreams and always remember that everything you have ever wanted is within you

"Your task is not to seek love for love

But merely to see and find

All the barriers within yourself

That you have built against it." Rumi

FEAR TO LOVE

An inner journey home

PROLOGUE

The air was warm and embraced us like a soft velvet blanket. Oh the feeling ... flying free in the sky. Nothing existed but love and joy. There was no past, no future, just a never ending series of perfect moments. We soared high today and my heart felt like it would explode with joy. We flew over Africa, over Rhodesia; though I didn't know that was what it was. Earth was just Earth. We dived lower and hovered over a beautiful white house that looked like a fairy castle. "That will be your home," he said, "when you return to earth. Wait for me there, until I return."

He showed me my parents; my mother-to-be was pregnant with me at the time. I watched her place her hands on her pregnant belly, and smile. She had been told she could never have children, and now there she was, waiting to give birth.

He told me what my purpose in returning was. He told me I would forget my truth, forget my home and forget the love. He warned me of the pains to come. "But fear not," he said, "for one day, before you return home, you will remember. You will remember, and you will teach what you know to others."

I looked into his beautiful, loving blue eyes. Light surrounded him. I memorised every feature.

I did not want to return to earth. The last few times had been painful and traumatic, and I feared this would be the same. I knew the past memories and patterns that were etched on my soul would be carried into this new life.

"I will help you as much as I can, my friend," he promised. "Listen for me, speak to me; I will always be with you. But beware — there will be tests. During those tests you will not hear me, you will forget."

I left my brothers and sisters in Heaven, and returned to Earth.

****

INTRODUCTION

"Maybe the journey isn't so much about becoming anything. Maybe it is about unbecoming everything that isn't really you so you can be who you were meant to be in the first place."

Anonymous

In 1979, a baby girl was born in Rhodesia. Her parents were dairy farmers on a beautiful farm called Melfort situated forty minutes south east of the capital, now called Harare. They had moved to Rhodesia in 1976 with the British Army, and had decided to stay.

When she was three years old the little girl told her parents that Jesus had flown with her over Melfort before she was born and said that it would be her home, and that her family would always be protected there. She also sang a song in a strange language. When her mother asked her what she was singing she replied, "It's Hebrew. Jesus taught it to me."

That little girl was me.

In 2013, my world crashed down around me when I found out that my now ex-husband, who I will refer to as J in this book, was having an affair. I had met him when I was nineteen. We had been married for thirteen years and we had a two-year-old daughter.

In 2014, I moved with my daughter from New Zealand to Belfast, Northern Ireland, where my sister, Vicky and her family lived. A ghost of my former self, I suffered from panic attacks, insomnia and depression.

Once I had recovered sufficiently, I moved into my own home with my daughter. I had never lived alone before.

One day, I looked in the mirror and asked the question: "Who am I?" I had absolutely no idea.

That question, that moment, saw the beginning of an inner journey that can only be described as a dark night of the soul. An inner winter.

Everything I had thought I was had disintegrated; dashed to pieces, scattered around me. The only way forward was to go within. So that is what I did.

It was not an easy journey. I waded through the kaleidoscope of memories that swirled through my mind, and all the emotions that went with them. I travelled back to early childhood, back to my beautiful home in Africa where I'd grown up. Back through the portal of my mind that I'd firmly shut when I left Zimbabwe in 2001; the farm invasions and subsequent troubles had meant it wasn't safe to stay. Back into the trauma of a relationship I'd remained in for too long.

In the deepest, darkest moments I shone a light on the walls around my heart; walls that had been encased in stone for many, many years.

As I travelled through the darkness I began to see that everything I had ever thought I was, was just an illusion; a collection of false beliefs that I'd collected along the way. But, underneath it all my true self was still there, untouched.

In this book, I share the inner places I visited and the insights and realisations that surfaced on my journey from fear to love. My hope in writing this book is that it will inspire you to make your own inner journey, if that is what you are called to do. That it will whisper to you to step into your power, embrace your truth, and shine as we are all meant to. That it will beckon you to step through your fear, and into love.

Everything you have ever wanted is within you, just waiting.

Much love,

Belinda xxx

PART ONE

SELF INQUIRY

"The most important relationship you can have is the one you have with yourself, the most important journey you can take is one of self-discovery. To know thyself, you must spend time with yourself, you must not be afraid to be alone. Knowing yourself is the beginning of all wisdom."

Aristotle

CHAPTER ONE
Who am I?

"We don't attract what we want, we attract what we are."

Wayne Dyer

It's surprising how many of us don't know who we are. We know who we are in terms of our roles and functions, but what about deeper than that? How many people know what is underneath? What their true nature is? What makes their soul sing? I know I didn't.

In all of us there is an inner child; an original or true self, an inner being of authenticity and truth; the heart of who we are. When we go through trauma that we can't process at the time the authentic self goes into hiding to escape the feelings and emotions associated with the event, and it forms defences to protect itself from the emotional pain. In other words, another part of us takes over to protect the authentic self. As we grow older and experience more trauma the inner child goes deeper and deeper into hiding, and more walls are built to protect the self.

There is a belief that the trauma that causes this has to be severe in order for someone to truly lose their sense of self. This is not the case at all. For some it can be just a single word, a single action that doesn't necessarily even appear violent, and the inner child retreats into a deep, dark hole, and the process of losing oneself begins. The inner child will only come out of hiding when he or she feels it is safe to do so. For some, that time never comes. For others it does.

That is what happened to me. I started off whole, as we all do, but as the years went by my inner child hid deeper and deeper; another part of me ran my life. There came a time when I had completely forgotten who I was. I was so distanced from my authentic self that I didn't know what my true thoughts, feelings, dreams or desires were.

In December 2013, I discovered my now ex-husband, J, was having an affair. I found out through checking his phone messages early one morning before he woke up. I'd known something wasn't right for months but I'd never had any proof, and he kept his phone by his side twenty-four hours a day. Until that day. The day he slipped up.

In that moment, my entire world crashed down and splintered into tiny fragments around me. I felt as though my heart had been grabbed in a vice-like grip by an iron hand and ripped straight out of my chest.

Disbelief, anger, shock, indignation, and pain cursed through my body. I remember thinking, or rather screaming, why me? How could he do this to me? I'd been a great wife. I'd given him a beautiful child. How could he have treated me this way? Disrespected me, broken the vows we had made so many years ago. How could he have lied so blatantly for months!

The marriage that I thought we had, the love that I thought we shared, was broken, over.

Around me, life continued as normal. My daughter woke up and needed to be cared for. She needed her mother. Yet, inside I was dying. If I hadn't had her, I'm not sure I would have made it through.

I had been married for thirteen years and so much of who I thought I was had been invested in my marriage. I'd given up so many of my own goals and dreams during that time; not because I was forced to but because I'd chosen to. Now that it was over I'd forgotten who I once was.

It was agreed that I would move to the UK where my sister and extended family lived because I had no other family in New Zealand. It was six months before that happened, and those six months were a living hell. I packed up and sold the family home, closed my business, and said goodbye to the world I'd known for twelve and a half years. My heart broke yet again when I had to find homes for our beautiful dog, and my adorable rescued cat.

I felt sick most of the time, and don't know what I would have done if it hadn't been for the love and support of friends, particularly my neighbour, Ellen. Ellen was my rock; the person I went to when I felt I couldn't continue. She was always there for me, ready to listen without judgement. I often found myself sitting in her kitchen with a cup of coffee, grateful for the comfort of her company. She would regularly take Lucy for me too so I had some space to myself. Lucy loved her like a grandmother and was always more than happy to visit her 'Lellie' as she called her.

In August 2014, I moved to Belfast, Northern Ireland with my daughter and moved in with my sister, Vicky, and her family. J moved over as well so our daughter would still have contact with her father.

I was a mess. I was having panic attacks, suffering from insomnia, and literally lived moment to moment. I couldn't drive. It was terrible. I was determined not to take any form of medication, and I never did. In time it became easier, and I felt better, but I knew I was far from healed.

Ten months later, I moved into my own place with my daughter. It may sound a bit daft to say I'd never lived alone before when in fact my daughter was with me, but that's what it felt like, as I'd always lived in my family home until I got married.

Afraid of the future, too scared to look at the past, I signed up for a course in corrective exercise coaching. I had always loved studying and over the years had done many courses in the field of natural therapy and fitness. I knew I had to make a living, and I had so little faith in myself I believed I needed to learn more before I could do this.

I focused my energy on the future, my studies, everything outside myself, and blocked the pain. It was a tactic I'd used for many years.

But this time it didn't work.

I remember sitting down to study one day, probably about two months into the course, and hearing a voice inside me say: 'no more courses'. What? I'd invested money and energy into it, I had my business plan sorted, plus I needed to support myself and my daughter! What on earth was going on? I did my best to ignore it, but it grew louder.

There was something about it that was vaguely familiar. I'd heard it before; a long, long time before, but I couldn't remember when.

I didn't know what to do. For days I kept going, trying to study, but the more I persisted and pushed along the path the more 'wrong' it felt. What was scaring me was that if I didn't carry on with the study and business, what would I do?

With my heart in my mouth, I cancelled all further courses, and I waited ... and waited.

Nothing happened, I just stopped studying. The pressure started to build. I felt tense, irritable, claustrophobic. I remember going into my room one day and just bursting into tears. I cried and cried and cried. Emotions I'd bottled up for months came bubbling to the surface. I realised that in staying with my family I hadn't given myself the space to heal; to cry when I needed to; to let go of my marriage. That emotional release brought a huge shift inside me. I went from fighting to avoid my inner turmoil to actually beginning to acknowledge it, and realise that what I needed ... was me.

I was a single mother, living alone with my little girl, and I had no idea who I was, and, what was even more frightening was that I couldn't remember if I'd ever known. I'd spent most of my life living in fear, trying to be what other people wanted me to be. I'd given away my power, hidden my feelings and lived in the shadows of those I put on pedestals above me.

****

CHAPTER TWO
Fear

"Everything you want is on the other side of fear."
Jack Canfield

Ever since I could remember, fear had dominated my consciousness. I was afraid of failure, afraid of being judged, afraid of being wrong, afraid of the future, and, as I can see now, afraid of my inner world. I gave up trusting my knowing a very long time ago.

If there was one thing I did know about myself, it was that I'd never paused long enough to look inside my own soul. I didn't know why, and it scared me. When my daughter was born, I allowed myself to go inwards briefly but soon after, the 'busyness' of life drew me away again and I lost the short-lived connection to my inner self.

Why? I asked. Why had I made my life so busy that I didn't know who I was? Why had I chosen to shut all that I was out? Was it because of my marriage? It hadn't been the happiest of relationships. Was it trauma from childhood? I'd certainly had my fair share of challenges, but who hadn't?

I became really curious. Who was Belinda? What made her soul sing? What was her true nature?

I was afraid of not being able to support my daughter. I knew I had to go on this inner journey and that it would mean I would have to turn inwards and stop worrying about money, but that was very hard to do.

I was also afraid that if I let myself go within I would somehow lose my grip on reality. I'd been through some traumatic times, I knew that, but I was so afraid that if going within was painful enough I might revert to some of my old coping mechanisms, such as alcohol abuse. Could I trust myself not to? I had to, my daughter depended on me and I couldn't jeopardise that.

I was like a bunny in the headlights; frozen to the spot, not sure where to start and not convinced I wanted to. Some of my most painful memories began to rear their ugly heads so I knew that no matter how scared I was, I absolutely had to take this journey and face the demons within.

****

CHAPTER THREE
Anger

"The more anger towards the past you carry in your heart, the less capable you are of loving in the present."
Woody Allen

I felt angry. I <u>was</u> angry; angry at life; angry at J for leaving me to raise our daughter alone, angry at myself for staying in our marriage too long, for not listening to my intuition many years before when the signs were clearly laid before me; alarm bells I'd ignored.

Fury was simmering with nowhere to go. It seeped into my daily life; boiling, bubbling, spilling over and burning everything in its path. I kept the lid tightly in place, but I knew I couldn't contain it forever. I knew I was simply burying the agonising grief I was too scared to confront.

It was around that time that I began to listen to a speaker called Marianne Williamson. I listened to her webinars every week and something about what she said began to sink in. She spoke of forgiveness. She spoke of anything that isn't love being a cry for love. She used the words, 'I can be hurt by nothing but my thoughts. I can change all thoughts that hurt.' I kind of got what she meant, but the pain went so much deeper than my day-to-day thoughts.

Her webinars were based on the book, *'A Course in Miracles,'* so I bought the book. It contains 365 lessons, one for each day of the year. Every day I would read one of the lessons and use the key words as a mantra to help me through whatever problems or emotions came up. I did this for eight months, and it worked well — for a while.

Initially, it helped me start the process of forgiving J, to look more clearly at the relationship, and to see why it had ended the way it did. I began to understand that forgiveness was something I should be doing for myself, and in so doing would be setting myself free.

But, it also brought up other stuff. There's a part of the book that reads: 'the past is gone, it can touch me not,' and whilst that helped me immensely in releasing my marital issues, I just couldn't apply it to my childhood. Something kept blocking me every time, but I couldn't find it.

My childhood was something I hadn't thought about in years; not since leaving Zimbabwe in 2001. Even before that I'd thought nothing about it at all. Why were the memories so deeply hidden? What was I running from? What was I so afraid of?

While I was living in Belfast with Vicky, the conversation turned inevitably to our childhood.

"You were never a happy child," she told me one day. Why was that? I had no idea. I knew happiness was something that I'd struggled to find all my life; could it have stemmed from my early years?

Once I'd started on that path, I knew I couldn't stop. If I did I would be turning my back on myself again, and I couldn't do that. Somehow, though the journey had only just begun, I had made a fledgling connection to my inner child, and I would never break it again. She needed me now; we were in this together.

****

CHAPTER FOUR
Guilt

"Guilt is the source of sorrows, the avenging fiend that follows us with whips and stings."
Nicholas Rowe

Once I'd given myself permission to discover who I truly was I became increasingly aware of the guilt that surfaced. Voices in my head kept saying: 'your feelings aren't important,'… 'get over yourself, you're too sensitive,'… 'don't be so selfish, who do you think you are?' I'd heard these voices many times before, and listened to them. But, this time I knew I had to choose differently, and in so doing I opened a chink, an invitation, and with it, a shift in perception.

Guilt is a complicated emotion. It stems from the pressures and expectations others put upon us that we then buy into and take upon ourselves. It's an emotion that I've encountered regularly throughout my life. We think guilt comes from doing something wrong, but it's much deeper than that. It goes back much further than what is happening at the time it's first recognised.

Deep-seated guilt prevents us from enjoying life or thriving emotionally. It often results in self-punishing, destructive behaviour initiated to combat the feelings.

Why did I feel guilty for being me? Why did I feel guilty for putting my feelings first? For choosing me, instead of constantly giving in to others? Where did all this stem from?

The inquiry grew. So many questions! So much to discover, much more than just the answer to the question: 'who am I?'

When I posed the question: 'where do I start, what do I need to do to embark upon this inner quest,' the word I heard was, 'surrender.' Surrender to everything. Just allow what needs to come up to rise to the surface to be healed, forgiven and released.

For as long as I can remember I have loved writing. It has always been a very healing process for me and a way to connect to my inner self. I've kept journals for many years and when I was in school I wanted to be a writer. I'd buried this dream for many reasons, but now it was time. I could see the book before my eyes. I knew this journey had to be set down in words. I didn't know when I started what the book would look like. Would it be a tragedy? Would I ever complete it? All I knew was that I needed to start.

****

PART TWO

SURRENDER

"You cannot reach for anything new if your hands are full of yesterday's junk."

Louise Smith

CHAPTER FIVE
The early years

"Why do people voluntarily repress themselves and adopt crippling defence mechanisms? It is not voluntary. It looks as if it is voluntary because by the time you become alert it is almost inside your blood and bones. But it is not voluntary - it is forced, it is violent."

Osho

This morning I meditated, and asked to remember. To remember the nature of who I am; to remember my music. I am taken into the energy of myself as a new-born baby. I feel love, I feel whole, and I feel complete. I can sense my parents' energy. They are so proud, so joyous and so content.

I am wrapped in a white woollen blanket. My green eyes are wide and sparkling with curiosity and life. All these new senses to explore; safe in my mother's arms.

I am handed over to a nanny. I peer at her and I sense she is not my mother. Where is my mother? I'm too young to understand, but I can sense, and I sense something is wrong.

In that moment the seeds of separation are planted, and a tiny, little part of my heart closes off.

For four years I had a full time nanny called Gladys. I don't remember her at all, but my mother tells me I adored her. She slept in our house when I was a new-born and took care of my every need. African women carry their babies on their backs, tied on with a blanket or sheet. That way their arms are free to carry on doing whatever they're doing. I was carried around like this until I could walk. Once I could walk, I was allowed to explore.

I saw my parents at certain times of the day. In the evenings my father would spend time with me. I don't really remember it but my mother said he would dance round the hall with me, a record of Bach or Mozart playing in the background. Classical music played a large part in my life. Both my parents were very musical. Daddy loved Nellie Melba who was one of the most famous singers of the late Victorian era and the early 20th century. Both my parents loved Bach, Beethoven and Mozart. My mother played the piano and some of my earliest memories are of her singing. I would sing too, when I was older. Usually in front of my parents' guests which was rather nerve wracking.

Melfort, a farm in Zimbabwe, was my home and as I grew I explored my surroundings. My parents had moved to Rhodesia in 1976, because my father had been posted there with the British Army. In 1978, they bought Melfort Farm, and in 1980, my father left the army to begin dairy farming.

There was something magical about Melfort. Built in the early 1900s, it was Cape Dutch in style. It had five bedrooms, a huge entrance hall, drawing room, dining room and all the other rooms a house usually has. Every bedroom had a large fireplace, as did the hall, dining room and drawing room. Every winter we would have a roaring fire in the hall and several dogs would gather to soak up the warmth. It welcomed you in, and almost seemed to talk to you. At least, that's what I felt. There were rumours that it was haunted, but I never saw or felt anything unpleasant.

I was aware of a lot of things as a little girl. Things that in later years I blocked from my memory. I used to feel the spirits of angels at Melfort. There were times when I thought I saw them, above the house, and in the garden. They were beautiful, and I loved being around them. I would spend hours in the huge gardens around the house, playing under the frangipani trees and in the bamboo; lost in an inner world of imaginings and joy. I had such a rich inner world, and I preferred being there than around people. I was called shy, reserved, but the truth of the matter was that my inner world was more fun, and felt much safer.

Before I was a year old my mother bought me a pony called Panda. Panda was as old as the hills, grey in colour and quiet as a lamb. I had a basket saddle that I was strapped into; like a small cane armchair with a girth. I've always thought it was that saddle that taught me to ride in an upright position. Secured onto Panda's back, I would be taken for rides by a groom who was usually on horseback too.

Panda didn't stay very long, he was replaced by Emily Puddleduck, a Shetland pony that clearly hated every moment of being ridden. She bit and bolted and had a shy that would unseat the most balanced of riders. She was my pony until I was about six years old.

When I was four Gladys left. Her husband had been given a job by my Godmother, so of course Gladys left too. There was a great hoo-ha about it all, and my father swore he would never speak to my Godmother again. I didn't understand and according to my mother I cried for days. I must've blocked it out for I have no memory of it whatsoever.

It was also the year that my sister Vicky was born, and I became very aware of how different my mother's interactions were with her compared to me. Vicky didn't have a full time nanny, my mother was much more involved with her day-to-day care than she had been with mine, and I was acutely aware of this. The memories now are vague, just images in my head, but I'm still aware of the emotions I felt. I remember feeling as if I was doing something wrong; that I was 'bad'. I wasn't aware what the emotion was then but later, of course, I see it must have been guilt.

Little children don't know how to process big emotions. What they want to do is cry, what they need is someone to tell them that they're loved no matter what they're feeling. I didn't get that. It wasn't my parents fault, they did the best they could with the resources they had, but I, as a four-year-old, couldn't possibly understand that. I did what little children do. I took it all personally, blamed myself for it, and bottled it up inside. I always seemed to upset my mother, and this became more and more apparent after Vicky was born. I was jealous of her; though I didn't understand that was what I felt at the time.

While I write now about my inner world I remember how happy I was as a girl of about three or four, and I ask myself what changed? What caused me to begin shutting down, to begin locking my heart away?

The first memory that comes up is the day of my sister's christening.

My granny was over from England and we were all getting ready for the special occasion. I was upstairs in my parents' room where my mother was getting Vicky and me ready. I said something, or did something, I can't remember what, but I remember being beaten with my hairbrush. I remember feeling devastated and having no idea how to express the overwhelming emotions I was experiencing. I ran to my granny for comfort and she cradled me in her arms. I hated the world that day. I wanted to run away, but there was nowhere to run. I had to pretend everything was fine; to smile for the guests and the photographs. I was too scared not to.

That day marked a pivotal point in my relationship with my mother. Its ramifications would lead eventually to the self-deprecating belief systems that would affect my relationships with others for many years to come. My filing cabinet of experiences was founded that day. I locked away part of my heart, and I didn't even realise until much later that I'd done it. As an incredibly sensitive and intuitive child, I could read people's emotions like a book and my mother's inner world scared me. I 'knew' that something was wrong.

As the quote by Osho asks, *'why do people voluntarily repress themselves and adopt crippling defence mechanisms?'* It is taught, and it is taught early. By the time we realise what has happened the coping mechanisms have become subconscious patterns we don't even realise we have. If we ever realise at all. Some people go through their entire life replaying them. I felt unloved that day. I felt attacked and therefore, under threat. I felt as if I wasn't wanted, wasn't good enough. I can see now, in hindsight, it was the first time I'd experienced guilt.

I tried so hard to be what my mother desired, but it's incredibly stressful for a child who feels she can do nothing right. My mother was always unhappy with me in those early years, shouting at me, calling me names, punishing me. I remember she would hold on to issues for days. Sometimes, if I'd done something particularly bad she would shut herself in her bedroom and refuse to come out. I would sit on the floor outside the room and beg her to forgive me. Those were terrifying times. When I was older and could write, I would slide apology letters under the door.

Children are about survival and having their needs met. I learnt fast what I needed to say, what I needed to do. I learnt to think before I said anything. To say what I knew she wanted me to say and not what I really felt. My feelings weren't important — at least that's what experience taught me. What was important was keeping the peace at all costs, or suffering the consequences.

When I look back, I realise my mother must have been very unhappy, but of course I didn't understand that, I thought it was all my fault. On one particular occasion I was outside with my father in the garden when we heard a cry from the bedroom window. My mother was hanging out, threatening to jump. "Don't worry, she'll never do it," said Daddy. But that along with other similar incidents haunted me for years.

My parents used to fight a lot and after I turned four they would use me as a mediator in their disputes. I was the peacemaker. I would plead with them to stop fighting and would relay messages between them when they refused to speak to each other. I remember meal times where I would sit between them and mediate the conversation. I had no choice; it was horrible.

I turned to my father more and more in the months and years that followed. He was a quiet man, similar in nature to me, and I was content to simply follow him around. I loved him very much, and I felt he understood and accepted me, unlike my mother. I remember many an afternoon sitting on his knee while he read me stories. It was he who first taught me to read, and to do my times tables. And it was he who told me I had to always be strong, that I was a soldier's daughter.

He would get up early in the morning and do stretches on the upstairs balcony, and I would get up at the same time and sit quietly in the corner watching the sunrise. The sunrise in Africa is the most beautiful process to watch. The birds sing to welcome in the new day. The air is rich with the sounds of dawn, the sounds of life pulsing through the land, inviting you to breathe deeply and fill your lungs with the energy of life. The air is warm and the sky is lit with exquisite colours that cast their glow on the land.

I would then go and get dressed before following him to the dairy in time for the morning milking.

He had given me my own cow, a Friesian-cross-Simmental called Fab. I adored Fab. She was slightly fluffy, and had the biggest, kindest eyes in the world. She would meander in to the parlour, usually towards the end of the milking, and walk into her bay. The cows were fed during milking and although a few of them had hobbles most of them were so tame there was no need.

Fab had the patience of a saint, quietly waiting whilst I fumbled around trying to milk her. There was an art to hand milking, which at five years old I hadn't quite mastered. There were many times when I ended up with milk in my eyes and all over my clothes!

The dairy smelt of cotton hulls and cow meal. Behind the milking bays was an area where the sacks of food were kept. My sister and I spent many an hour climbing them, content in our own little world. I was always fascinated by the medicine cupboard. It had a funny smell to it. Throughout my life I've always been very sensitive to smells. They can take me to an exact time and place in my mind, triggering memories in an instant. Whenever a cow was sick I would help the dairy foreman, Isaiah, treat it. By the time I was eight I could apply bandages and dressings quickly and effectively, and was comfortable administering injections.

Every two weeks the farm vet, Bruce Wells, made his routine visit and I would shadow him, fascinated by his vast array of medicines and equipment. I wanted to learn to help animals like he did.

We had cats at the dairy, many cats. I always wanted to touch the kittens. I recall one day seeing two little balls of fluff by the medicine cupboard. I knelt down to reach for them when out of nowhere the mother appeared, tail in the air and all claws bared. She went for me, scratching my legs badly. I screamed and ran. Needless to say, I avoided kittens after that.

When I wasn't shadowing my father, I would be at the stables. Horses were my greatest love. They were my friends, my confidants and my source of comfort. I rode them but also just loved to sit with them. Most of my day would be spent at the stables. If I wasn't around the horses I could be found in the tack room. I loved to polish the tack. The smell of the leather was so comforting and as I polished it my thoughts would wander to images of riding in competitions all over the world. I had moved on from Emily Puddleduck by the time I was six and now had a pony called Picollo. He was black, elderly and wise. He was much bigger than Emily but that never worried me. Emily's unpredictable behaviour under saddle meant I was now a confident and well balanced rider! Much to Emily's delight she'd become a brood mare, and had joined my mother's pony stud.

The stud comprised a beautiful Welsh Section B stallion called Powys, and a few mares of different breeds. Powys had a glorious flowing white mane and tail and often reminded me of what I imagined Pegasus would look like. The idea behind the stud was to breed then sell, but most of the time the foals matured and never left Melfort. As my sister and I grew up we would start them when they were old enough and compete them in the local shows. I remember at one stage having about five ponies to exercise each day! It was marvellous, I would get up early in the morning and have them all exercised by 10 am. My father was not so taken by the idea as he believed the stud was a business, however for the most part he would turn a blind eye. My mother's soft spot for horses became known within the industry and often she would take in animals people couldn't find homes for. Melfort became a bit of a horse haven, and the numbers grew. About once a year my father would put his foot down and some would go on the market, but it was just a matter of time before they were replaced.

****

CHAPTER SIX

The little church on the farm

"Peace is always beautiful."
Walt Whitman

At the far end of Melfort there was a little church that belonged to the farm, and we went to the service there every Sunday. I loved going because we would dress up in our Sunday best. When I was a child we didn't get new clothes or go shopping very often so it was such a treat to wear my best dress and shoes every weekend.

I remember many a Sunday sitting next to my parents on the right hand side at the front. My father would take one of the readings each week and I loved to listen to him. I didn't understand or follow everything that was going on, but I felt spirit in that church. It was the same sense I connected to when I was alone in the garden or with the horses. I talked to it and in my head I had an image of what it looked like. It was a man with long red hair, a beard and blue eyes. He was dressed in a flowing white robe. There was something very familiar about him.

To this day I can still remember the hymns that were sung. I loved to sing and though I rarely sang in church I would follow the hymns in my head when I was alone. Two of the ladies in the congregation were amazing singers, Ronnie Magden and Rhoda Tibbs, and their voices would rise above everyone else's in the small congregation. Ronnie Magden used to play the organ. When I was little it was a real organ, but later it was upgraded to an electric keyboard that created much excitement amongst our small community as it was quite flash. Rhoda Tibbs was a gentle, softly-spoken lady. She was always very kind to me, and reminded me of a bird, a little shy and flighty.

When the congregation grew, my father built two extensions on to the church, one at the back, and one with a beautiful stained glass window at the front.

Many years later, when I was much older, I would borrow the key for the church and go there on my own. I would sit quietly and listen. Or cry. Or talk. It was a very healing place and I treasured my times there.

It's funny, as I sit and write this on a rainy Wednesday evening, the church that I currently live next to is having hymn practice. Some of the hymns I remember from our little church at Melfort, and my heart feels deeply moved.

I'm transported back to that little church at Christmas; a very special time for me when I was a little girl, and for the four of us as a family. There was always a service on Christmas Eve at 6 pm. Beautiful Christmas carols were sung and it was a warm-hearted, spiritual occasion. After the service we would go home and sit as a family in the drawing room. We would eat mince pies and have a glass of sherry. Well, my sister and I didn't have sherry until we were older, but my mother and father did. It was such a tradition we continued it until I grew up. The stockings would be hung by the fireplace and my mother would read us, *'The Night Before Christmas,'* by Clement Clarke Moore. To this day I remember the poem word for word, and I still read it regularly to my own daughter.

On Christmas morning my sister and I would go into our parents' room for morning tea and prayers. Two very excited little girls we were. This was, in fact, an every-morning routine. The cook would bring the tray upstairs at 6 am and we would get up and go into their room followed by a clowder of hungry and slightly feral cats. The cats were given saucers of milk first. There was actually a separate jug of milk just for them. Once they were happy we would have tea followed by prayers. The difference on Christmas morning was that it was followed by present opening and stocking investigation.

Afterwards we would have a family breakfast, followed by the giving of gifts to the staff. They would all congregate outside the kitchen and my father would give a Christmas speech, thanking them for their hard work and support during the year. Each family would be given a hamper of food, which always included the favourites — a 50 kgm sack of mealie meal and several bags of Kapenta. Kapenta are small fresh water sardines that were dried and well salted. The Africans loved them. Vicky and I always gave away our unwanted toys and clothes to the children. There were never enough for all of them of course, but we did our best. It was something we felt drawn to do. Growing up in Africa meant we had a deep understanding of how little some people had.

At about 11 am we would get into the Mercedes, which was spit-polished for the occasion, and drive to Pauline and Sandy Ward's home in Harare. Sandy was my father's ex-army friend. They'd been posted together at Llewellin Barracks in Bulawayo in 1976 when he and mother had first moved out to Zimbabwe.

Sandy was a light-hearted, funny man. He would always tease us, and as being teased was something neither Vicky nor I were used to, it would take us greatly by surprise. He used to have a trick of pretending to steal one's nose; it took me many visits to get my head around that.

Pauline was frightfully English, had a very pukka accent and the kind of personality that demanded instant respect. I was a little scared of her. She was always nice, but one got the impression that the slightest accident or slip up would cause great trouble. She had a very aristocratic nose and would look down it over the top of her narrow rimmed glasses in a way that made me feel incredibly small.

Their home was immaculate, very different from Melfort which was always in a state of chaos. They had a dog, an outside dog, and a very posh looking cat with a collar. Not a single thread was out of place in that house. It intrigued me how such perfection could exist in a home. I liked to explore every room when I was there just to see if it was as perfect as I remembered it from the previous year.

The dinner table was always laid out in preparation for the silver service. Vicky and I had our own little table out of sight of the adults. We were not particularly enamoured by this but obviously said nothing. Their cook was called Philip, or 'Phileeep' as Pauline called him. He was dressed in executive chef attire with the black pants and bowtie. At dinner time Pauline would ring the silver bell and Phileeep would appear with a silver tray. The meal was out of this world every year.

In the afternoon, Vicky and I would play in the garden and when we were old enough; swim in the pool. Left to our own devices we explored, laughed and loved life. The Wards had fancy lilos in their pool. Although it was a very serious, frightfully posh affair those Christmas days were very special. I have such fond and happy memories of those times with my family. I felt closer to my mother and there was a sense of joy and unity. To this day, Christmas reminds me of those special times and my heart warms when I look back.

****

CHAPTER SEVEN
Gift or curse?

"Angels walk among us, you may not always see them, you may feel them, hear them, or just know they are there."
Carmen Jordan

Before I left my daughter at Nursery this morning, I was watching her playing with her friends, and I was enchanted by the way they interacted with each other. There was no sense of separation, no self consciousness, just a pure expression of self. The realisation hit me that I'd never felt that as a child. Ever. I recognised it when I worked with the animals, especially the horses, but never with my peers.

I'd always been acutely aware of being very different to other children. I could feel things and sense things that they could not. Where I was content to sit in silence and listen to the sounds of nature, they wanted to run and shout and play. They also seemed to take a delight in picking on the weakest in the group which for me was horrifying because I could feel the pain of the bullied child as if it were my own. Feeling the pain of others haunted me as a child. I had no one to talk to about it and there were many nights when I didn't sleep for fear of the nightmares that would come.

When I was about five years old my father took me with him to Harare to see a lawyer about some important farm business. In the city centre there were beggars on the street, many of whom were the victims of bombings during the war. I remember on that particular day seeing a blind woman. She was dressed in rags and singing in a low, mournful voice. In front of her was a rusty old bowl that had a few cents in it. She had a baby with a runny nose; small and undernourished. I was very traumatised by this sight. I wanted to take her home, feed her, care for her. It hurt me physically and emotionally to listen to her song; I could feel what she'd been through. For days I felt haunted by her soul, as if it were pleading for help. I had no idea how to deal with those painful feelings. No one else seemed to feel it. Was it just me?

It wasn't just the blind woman, it was anyone and everyone that I came into contact with. It was as though I could see straight through them, right into whatever their deepest pain and fear was. I could sense it in my parents, and it terrified and appalled me. I looked up to them to protect me, yet I could see how vulnerable they themselves were. I didn't know what to do, so I talked to the 'presence' inside myself. The 'presence' was a warm, strong energy in the centre of my chest. It was light and it comforted me.

I also turned to the horses. Those strong, accepting beings brought me immense peace. I would often run away from the house, especially if my parents were fighting, and hide in a stable.

I didn't know if other people talked to an inner presence. No one ever mentioned it.

It's funny how memories come back to you when you allow them in. I'm taken into the garden at Melfort at about three years old. I remember feeling angels all around me. One of my favourite hiding places was under the frangipani tree. I could feel them strongly there. They were always so peaceful, so clear and so joyful.

I don't remember exactly when I stopped being aware of those feelings. Perhaps it began at my sister's christening. In closing down a part of my heart I shut them out to a large extent, although an awareness of them remained for a few more years to come.

****

CHAPTER EIGHT
Springvale

"Mirror mirror don't you see? What you show is ruining me."
Anonymous

Just before my sixth birthday it was decided that I should go to school. I was terrified, especially as it was a weekly boarding school. Why did they want to send me away? I never asked. I wasn't allowed to question. I had to do what I was told. I remember my mother packing my black trunk, and being bought a suitcase for the first time. My mother painted my name and address on the lid of the trunk and I remember thinking at the time that it was a bit like Paddington Bear. Perhaps I would get lost, be returned home quickly, and avoid school altogether.

The day arrived and I was driven to Springvale. We drove into the forecourt of the school in our old, white 1965 Mercedes. Around us were new cars, confident looking children, and smartly dressed parents.

A large African matron walked us up the stairs to the dormitory and I was shown my bed. It was advised that parents didn't 'hang around' too long, so we said our farewells and they left. I stood for a moment feeling so small in the huge room with my trunk and suitcase by my bed. The matron was still in the room, but I hardly noticed. Fear and grief welled up inside me and I lay on my bed and bawled my eyes out.

A male voice interrupted my tears. "Belinda Bennetts if you don't stop crying I'll give you something to cry about." I rolled over and saw the headmaster glaring at me. He was tall and broad and terrifying. I rolled back over and cried even harder out of sheer terror.

I felt a thud on the back of my neck, and heard a crack at the same time. In shock I fell silent. "I told you!" he shouted, storming out of the room.

My head ached and I was bewildered. Why had he hit me; he didn't even know me. I was petrified but there was no one to help me. In that instant I shut off another part of my heart; something inside me died. I knew myself to be abandoned and helpless. How could my parents have just left me; once again unloved and unwanted. There must be something very wrong with me, I thought. I am obviously not good enough for anybody.

Deep in my subconscious, core beliefs of being unworthy and deserving only to be punished were being laid down.

A miserable year followed during which I managed to be a good school girl and do what I was told, but I was never happy. I kept my distance from the other children; the defences I had built were strong and there was no way anyone was going to get through them. Plus, they were so different to me. They always seemed to know what to say, how to have fun, and how to play. I didn't. I would watch groups of girls playing together, laughing, talking about stickers, hair and the latest toys, and I wished I could fit in. But I never had the latest toys. My parents didn't know their parents. Their parents drove new cars, were young and trendy, whereas mine were much older and didn't dress the same or have the latest 'stuff.'

Of course, there was more to it than that. They didn't see things like I did. They were competitive and cruel. I would watch them picking on those that were weaker than them and I could feel the pain of the child being picked on. But I could also feel the pain of those doing the bullying. They weren't happy either; they didn't like doing those nasty things. They were doing it out of fear. I knew this, but I didn't know what to do about it. So I bottled it all up inside.

I began to hate that I was different. I didn't feel special, I felt like some sort of freak. I knew others could sense I wasn't like them and nothing I could do would change that. Why was I like this? Why could I sense these things? Why couldn't someone just make me normal! I became more and more withdrawn. I didn't believe there was anyone else like me out there, and I felt incredibly lonely. My intuition turned into a curse. I had such a rich inner world of images, feelings and connections to things that were not of this world, and I had no idea how to disassociate from it and live in the real world. Or integrate the two.

I developed deep-seated feelings of guilt and loathing just for being me. I would go home for the weekends and sometimes I would try to talk to my mother. But she was in her own emotional pain so never really had time for me. All I seemed to do was upset her, so I kept away. My father had always told me to be strong therefore I couldn't talk to him either. Vicky picked up on it. She may have been younger but she was very sensitive too and she knew I was deeply unhappy. She often asked my mother not to send me back.

Eventually my parents realised that boarding school wasn't working for me when I became more and more subdued and dejected.

So I was removed from Springvale and my parents found me a private tutor, a wonderful elderly lady called Mrs Pickard. She lived in a tiny flat quite close to the farm and had a small garden in front that was full of pansies. Pansies were my favourite flowers as a child. They looked like they had smiling faces that turned up towards the sun. She was a warm, kind lady and always gave me a slice of fruit loaf with lemon curd on it for break. I was often reminded of my granny when I was with her.

The three years that followed were the happiest of my childhood. My days were spent riding my ponies, roaming free on our beautiful farm and, at last, actually enjoying learning from Mrs Pickard.

****

CHAPTER NINE
Memories of England

"And then my heart with pleasure fills, and dances with the daffodils."
William Wordsworth

My father was English and my mother was Irish. Most years we would travel to the UK to see my grandparents and half brothers.

My granny on my mother's side was called Hilda. I called her Granny Gaga. She lived in a little cottage with a thatched roof on Gracious Street, in Selborne, Hampshire. She was an artist and a wood engraver. I adored her. She taught me to sew and knit, and to this day I love making things. She also taught me how to draw and paint and I have many fond memories of times spent in her art studio, which was a converted bedroom in her cottage. There were three easels in the room that held art works at various stages of development. Below the window was a wooden chest upon which her large array of pencils and Windsor and Newton watercolour paints sat. The room had a beautiful warm feel to it, and I treasured my times there with Granny. She was a patient teacher. She would carefully demonstrate how to mix the delicate colours with just enough water then carefully apply them to the paper. I was fascinated. During one visit she gave me my very own Windsor and Newton palette. I was thrilled and took very great care of it. I painted flowers mostly, pansies in particular. Sometimes we would walk to the meadow together and sketch. There was a little stream through it and many wild flowers grew there. Sometimes Vicky would join us, but often it was just Granny and me.

Granny Gaga was a very colourful person. She wore bright dresses teamed with a hat that sported either a brooch or a coloured band around it. Whatever the colour was it would match her stockings perfectly. It amazed me how many different coloured stockings she had! Green, pink, blue, purple, orange — a vast spectrum. They were all kept together in a drawer that contained lavender bags. To this day the smell of lavender reminds me of her.

Granny Gaga had never had her ears pierced, instead she wore screw-on or clip-on earrings. Again, the colours of the rainbow and all the hues in between could be found in her jewellery box. Daily, she would carefully select a pair to match her outfit. It fascinated me as a child. Often I would ask to look through her jewellery and try things on.

Her little cottage was cosy and intimate. After the vastness of Melfort I found this absolutely delightful. I always felt instantly at home there, in fact in England generally. There was none of the 'wildness' of Africa, and whilst I loved the wildness it was comforting to be in a place that felt so contained. I was fascinated by the milk — delivered in glass bottles with gold tops to the front door every morning. I was, obviously, accustomed to milk because we had cows, but this seemed so suburban, and I loved it. The milk tasted quite different too, probably because it was pasteurised and it was delivered by a real live Postman Pat. I wanted a life like that; one with no dramas.

We weren't able to stay in Granny's cottage because it was too small. Instead we stayed in an hotel called The Queens about a five-minute walk away. Back in those days, people were allowed to smoke indoors and my memories of The Queens consist of the aroma of freshly brewed coffee mixed with stale tobacco. It sounds unpleasant but it wasn't. It was like a warm embrace transporting you to a different world.

Across from The Queens was The Wakes, now the Gilbert White museum. We visited the museum many times. It had a slow, historical feel to it, and I remember walking around Gilbert White's house feeling as if I were being watched. It was both eerie and fascinating at the same time. I was very sensitive to energy, to vibes; I could 'read' a room as soon as I entered it.

Granny Gaga had a silver biscuit tin in her sitting room that always contained an assortment of luxury biscuits from Marks and Spencers. The funny thing was although they were meant to be luxury they were always rather awful and seemed slightly stale. Not that I would have ever dared to say anything!

She also had a love of strong peppermints. Altoids was the brand. They came in a tin, a silver tin. I used to ask for the empty tins and I would keep them for all my treasures. I was a collector of sorts, a hoarder really. My biggest collection was birds' eggs. I never took them from their nests, they were only ever the unbroken ones that I'd found on the ground. I would carefully make a hole at each end and blow the yolk out. Then the egg would be placed in a box on some cotton wool.

From the end of the road at Granny's cottage you could catch the bus to Alton and we did this often. My parents would take us to toy stores and coming from Zimbabwe these was like Aladdin's caves. Lots of shiny new things! My parents didn't have a lot of money but they always got us something. We would go clothes shopping too and be kitted out for most of the year ahead. Mother liked to buy us clothes from the op shops — Oxfam, Spastics and so on. I guess because we grew so fast there was no point getting us new clothes, but I didn't see it like that as a child. I thought it meant we were poor. Those shops gave me the creeps too. I could sense the people that had worn the clothing before and it felt weird.

When we weren't at Granny's we were in Hastings, East Sussex with my Granddad, Dennis. My father's father. He was a wonderful man, and I loved our visits to see him. He lived close to the sea, in fact you could see it from the bottom of his garden; most exciting when you came from a land-locked country! Often, during our stays, my half brothers would come down to see us. During one stay one of my brothers — I have five — and his family came down from Southport. As they hardly ever saw us they had brought presents. Not just one present but a big, black, bin bag filled with gifts!! I had never seen so many presents at one time!

It was in Hastings that I saw my first badger. One of my half brothers was staying at the same time as us and before going to bed he'd help me put food out for it.

In the middle of the night he woke me and we sat quietly watching through the window as the badger came to eat. I was amazed at how little it was. I'd always imagined badgers to be huge.

Many days were spent exploring the beach. It was a stony beach but I didn't mind. I loved searching for starfish in the rock pools and I would then throw them back out to sea. Hastings had some gorgeous quaint little shops, and was famous for the rock candy that we called 'Hastings Rock'.

One year we visited Hastings Castle and St Clement's Caves. The Castle I loved. I was not quite so taken by the caves. They were rather creepy, and their connection to the dark and bloody days of smuggling along the Sussex coast in the 17th and 18th centuries was disturbing. A famous tourist attraction, they were designed to show a clear picture of what went on all those years ago. The torture chambers and fake remnants of human life sent chills down my spine. I was relieved when we left and went on to visit the village of Rye.

Once the haunt of smugglers and highwaymen, Rye is made up of ancient buildings, cobbled streets and secret passages. I instantly loved it. We bought the biggest soft toy I'd ever seen there. It was a badger, and for many years it sat on the bottom of my bed.

They are such happy memories, my memories of England. I know my mother wanted to take us to Northern Ireland too but my father wouldn't allow it because he didn't think it was safe.

Although I adored Melfort, part of me wanted to live in England. It was the warmth of the people, and the cosiness of the houses that made me feel safe. In Zimbabwe you never knew what was coming next.

I missed my granny very much when we left. I knew she understood me. We would write to each other every month, and I couldn't wait to get to the post office to collect her letters.

I remember one year she sent me a series of cut-out postcards. These are cards that show designs that have to be cut out and folded to create a building; very similar to what used to be found on the back of cereal boxes. There's no glue involved. The only things required are scissors, small fingers and patience. This particular series was of the different types of English architecture such as Tudor and Georgian. I loved making them up and would write and tell her about them. I had a beautiful collection at the end of it, a complete English village with a church and a windmill.

****

CHAPTER TEN
The happy years

"We don't remember days, we remember moments."
Cesare Pavese

When I was about seven we had a swimming pool about two hundred and fifty metres away from the house, but its changing rooms had been turned into a cottage. So, when I was eight my father built another pool in the front garden.

The first tenants in the ex-swimming pool changing rooms were the Cookes. Vic and Juliette. Vic was an alcoholic, though I didn't understand what that meant at the time. His wife was a gentle, kind lady who loved to bake, sew and do crafts. I became quite close to her over the years they lived at Melfort. I remember Vicky and I making scented candles with her. We would collect as many candles as we could find in Melfort and take them over with us. They would all be melted down in a cooking pot. A couple of drops of essential oil were added and the wax was poured into a mould with a piece of string through it. It was simple but such fun! She had a warm, loving nature and around her I felt safe. I don't remember talking to her a lot, but I do remember being at her house as much as I could. She used to make me wrap around skirts in bright colours which I loved.

Not long after they'd moved in Juliette asked my mother if she could convert our old donkey cart into a mobile shop from which she would sell jams, crafts and cakes. Mother loved this idea and the old wooden cart was transformed into a quaint little store that was towed to the road side every weekend by the tractor. Our farm was literally off the main road so loads of people drove past.

We put things in it too, for instance African crafts that some of the staff made and certain second hand things from the house. It was such fun, I used to sit at the bottom of the drive with Juliette for hours. We called the place where the cart was parked the Crystal Patch, because we would find beautiful smoky quartz crystals in the ground there. In between customers I would dig in the dirt and unearth treasures to add to my collection. I often imagined finding a huge one that was worth a lot of money — but it never happened.

In 1988, my Granddad died and it was Juliette that held me together. He'd been staying with some family in Australia, and was visiting us en route to Hastings.

It was a beautiful hot day in March and Granddad was lying on a swing sofa in the garden. My father popped out to check on him and found him barely conscious. We took him to hospital immediately, but he passed away a few days later and I was devastated. Even worse, I wasn't allowed to go to his funeral. Both my sister and I were left with the Cookes and Juliette did her best to console us. Vicky was a bit too young to understand — but I did. That was my first experience of losing someone I loved.

After the Cookes left in 1988, Charlie Hewat and Julie Edwards, otherwise known as the Rhino girls, moved in. I was rather in awe of them. They had cycled from the UK to Zimbabwe — 22,000kms — to raise awareness and funds for the fight against rhino poaching. I spent a lot of time around them, Julie in particular. She rode horses so immediately I felt we had a bond and I would let her ride one of my favourites and take her on the best hacks on the farm. She also played the guitar, and I remember many an evening sitting round a fire listening to her sing. John Denver's *'Take me home Country Road'* was always a favourite. I would sit in silence absorbing it all and listening to the stories the others around the fire told.

Charlie and Julie became great friends with neighbours of ours, Pat and Marion Curry. They had a game park and also a tannery. We were allowed to drive though the game park whenever we wanted, and ride the horses through it too. Looking back, I realise how lucky I was to be able to ride amongst the wild animals; to walk with zebras, giraffe, impala and water buck. The freedom we had living in Africa in those days is something that is hard to describe.

Pat had a small cottage by the edge of the river that ran through the game park and we often used to go there for braais which are like barbeques. There was just a small fence around the building and the animals were free to come as close as they wished. One day I had just finished lunch when a young zebra approached the fence. I spent two hours sitting quietly waiting for it to come up to me. Patiently, I waited for it to become braver. Suspiciously, it watched me for an eternity before being willing to come closer. Finally, it came so close I could almost feel its breath, and our eyes met, but I knew if I tried to touch it, it would run. Close enough was good enough for me.

Sometimes on a Sunday, my parents would invite some of the local farmers and the congregation from our Church round for a braai. The trays would be prepared, the garden boy would light the fire in preparation for cooking, and my father would concoct the punch; a fruit punch which was mixed in a huge pottery urn. I loved those days helping my father. It was my job to collect the mint from the vegetable garden and it always smelled delicious.

The braai was quite an ordeal as my parents didn't often have visitors. The cook would be in his finest white uniform and for hours the kitchen would be a hive of activity. Our cook at the time was called Arnold. He'd been batman to one of my father's friends in the army and was the most incredible cook. Unfortunately, he was also a bit of a thief. I remember my mother coming home one day hollering that she'd just caught Arnold biking down the road wearing her sunglasses. She'd flagged him down and demanded to know where he got the glasses, to which he replied, "Ah, sorry, Medem," and handed them back. She said she didn't much fancy them after he'd been wearing them so she let him keep them.

Because my parents were older when they had us there were never any other children at these social get-togethers. I never minded. I was happy just to observe.

When I look back I realise that drinking alcohol was a huge part of the culture then. I remember many a time the guests would have drivers with them to take them home when they were wobbly. My father would often fall asleep afterwards on the swing sofa in the garden whilst the staff cleared everything away.

Those were happy days, carefree days. Days where we lived each moment fully and never worried about what the future would bring.

****

CHAPTER ELEVEN
The winds of change

"To all things there is a time and a season for every purpose under heaven."
Ecclesiastes 3:1

In 1989, the Rhino girls left and my sister's godfather, Andrew Fuller moved in. Andrew had been a farmer in Marondera for many years, but had decided to down scale. To say he was a character would be an understatement. He arrived along with some ancient Massey Fergusson tractors, five vicious-looking black dogs, and as much of his farm equipment as he could fit on the acre that made up his new home.

He didn't pay any rent; he would help us on the farm instead. The swimming pool that had once been clean and functioning was repurposed as a fish pond and bream were bred.

Andrew was an alcoholic. Whether it had started through boredom from living alone or as a result of traumas in the past I never knew, but drink he did.

He'd been in the British Army and sometimes, when he was on his fifth or sixth gin and tonic, he would mention conspiracies that he'd been involved in.

In 1991, a book called '*The Feather Men*' by Ranulph Fiennes was released. It was the story of four British soldiers who were assassinated by a hit squad known as 'The Clinic.' The murders took place over a 17 year-period and were carried out on the instructions of a Dubai Sheikh. Andrew claimed to have been involved with this in some way, though he never elaborated. He seemed genuinely afraid to talk about it but assured us it was the cause of his drinking.

Sometimes at night he would get so drunk he would fire shots into the night sky. Sometimes the shots were randomly aimed towards our house and the bullets would ricochet off the roof! My mother would simply harrumph muttering, "Oh dear, there goes poor Andrew again," and no more would be said. He never apologised the next day, he probably didn't even remember he'd done it.

He spent his days tinkering with his tractors and cultivating a large vegetable garden. He always dressed as though he had no money at all, and I often wondered if he ever bathed. He always looked covered in engine oil and rather wild. I think looking back I was slightly scared of him.

It was around the same time that my godmother, Pam, moved into another one of our cottages — my father loved building; over the years he built six.

It was godmother Pam who'd 'stolen' my nanny, Gladys, many years before, but that had all been forgiven and forgotten; Gladys had moved on, so Pam moved in.

Pam and Andrew had known each other for years and Pam had always fancied Andrew. Why was beyond me, but each to his own. On a Saturday evening Pam and Andrew would come round to our house for dinner. It was always a fancy affair and everyone dressed up. My mother and Pam wore beautiful kaftans and my father and Andrew wore shirts and ties. My sister and I loved these evenings. I would wear what I presumed was an old bridesmaid's dress and looking back we must've looked like something out of a Jane Austin book but we never saw it that way.

World domination was plotted on those nights. My mother used to say that father had grand ideas for Melfort. His dream was to open a game park one day and have a tourist resort. Melfort would have been perfect.

The finest wines would be brought out and my sister and I would watch the adults grow louder and drunker. My parents never drank too much, neither did Pam, but Andrew never knew when to stop. I remember he had false teeth. The drunker he got the more he would wiggle the teeth in his mouth. I would watch in horrified fascination as they dropped down. I would try desperately not to laugh hoping for the sake of his dignity they wouldn't end up in his wine glass.

Unfortunately, Andrew became argumentative and aggressive when he was drunk and many Saturday evenings ended with him being escorted home by an ever patient and adoring Pam.

****

CHAPTER TWELVE
The people of Africa

"Here I am, where I belong."
Karen Blixen, Out of Africa

We lived like kings in Africa. We had staff to cater for our every need and because of this we had all the time in the world to pursue whatever we wanted. I never really thought about it then — how much freedom we had. It was just the way things were. The Africans needed work, needed to feed their families, and as farmers we provided jobs for many. My parents were always very kind to the staff and helped them as much as they could. Our staff were loyal for the most part and respected my father.

I remember many of them today and realise that they are probably dead now. Some through old age; others from AIDS. Zimbabwe today has one of the highest HIV rates in the world. I didn't really see it when I was a young girl but from about the age of fourteen it became more noticeable.

The local people where I grew up were the Shona. They were a gentle, kind race. They're a group of Bantu people that originated in Zimbabwe and other neighbouring countries. It's thought that the term 'Shona' was invented in the late 19th century by the Zulu king Mzilikazi. King Mzilikazi was a southern African king who lived from 1790 to 1868. He was the founder of the Matabele Nation, Matabeleland, which became Rhodesia and is now Zimbabwe.

Between the 11th and 15th centuries a city was built that is now known as Great Zimbabwe. Scientific research has shown that the city was built by the Shona, and it is the largest pre-European stone-built enclave in Africa. I used to visit the ruins often while I was growing up. Vicky would usually come with me and we would camp there at our peril for the campsite was also home to a large number of over-confident vervet monkeys who were expert food thieves.

There was something very mystical about the ruins. I could feel the spirits of the people who had lived and died there so many years before. There was a long, steep staircase to the top and I could almost hear the quick, light footsteps of those that traversed them centuries before.

I never really thought about the fact that, as whites, we were in the minority. We just got on with things. When you grow up with something you don't question it, you just accept it as the status quo.

I remember we had a groom called Alec. Alec used to come with us to all the horse shows, and he was a great rider. On competition day Alec would groom my pony to perfection. He would plait its mane and tail and follow me to the ring, duster in hand. If I won, he took total credit for it. If I lost, he would sulk. Because we bred ponies I had to break them in when they were old enough and prepare them for the shows. Alec was my right hand man. Any pony that showed signs of being difficult Alec would get on first. "Let me, madam Belinda," he would say and I would step aside, much relieved.

Alec would bring a bag of blackened corn seeds to work with him. Charred and crispy they smelt delicious. At morning tea time all the staff would gather at the kitchen door and we would provide them with sandwiches and tea. Alec would share his corn with me. I never thought as a little girl that the corn was probably very precious to him, never realised how generous he was being in sharing it with me.

Never in my life had I seen sandwiches as thick as the ones the staff had at tea time. Bread was never pre-sliced in those days. Our cook would cut slices as thick as one and a half inches! The inside would be smothered in margarine and a rather revolting looking red jam called Sun jam which was a favourite. It would all be washed down with sweet milky tea from a metal mug. They would sit on old drums and rickety chairs and enjoy their break. Most of them started work at six in the morning so must have been hungry by ten.

We had a gardener called Gideon. Well, he was a gardener/dog carer. My mother ran a cattery and boarding kennels and Gideon was in charge. We had about sixteen dogs of our own of varying shapes and sizes. Most of them were outside dogs, some slept in the house. My father hated them in the house but somehow they managed to sneak in every night. We had four Afghans as part of the pack. They slept on the veranda in huge cane baskets on old horse blankets. During the full moon they would howl. I remember once we had a visitor staying and the poor person nearly had a heart attack one night, fearing the Banshees had arrived when the Afghans broke into their raucous moon salute. The only thing that broke their reverie was rustling newspaper as close to them as possible. Something about the noise the paper made caught their attention and shut them up.

Gideon, the gardener, smoked tobacco rolled up in old newspaper. I would watch in fascination as he crushed the tobacco — nothing like the loose tobacco you get today — and roll it into the paper before licking it to stick it down. He had virtually no teeth and the ones he did have were broken and blackened. He had a habit of chewing the ends of matches. He would chew them so much that they ended up looking like fans, which he would then spit out and leave randomly all over the place.

Shadrek was our mechanic, and a dodgy mechanic he was too. My father knew nothing about engines and fixing things, and I don't think he wanted to either. Shadrek was adamant he knew all. He was a tall man from a different tribe to the Shona. He was an Ndebele. The Ndebele were a tribe that began when a Zulu chief broke away from King Shaka in the early 19th century. They were lead by Mzilikazi who lead his warriors into a battle for the chiefdoms of Southern Ndebele. They conquered the chiefdoms and this is where the name and identity of the kingdom came from. The tribe were known for being more aggressive than the Shona. But Shadrek was a kind man, and I spent many a day following him round the workshop area. I loved to make things and

Shadrek was my go-to person. He would help me with nails and screws, sawing wood and cutting wire.

One of my biggest projects was a mouse house. I spent hours putting it together and was very proud of the results. I liked to make sure my projects turned out as perfectly as possible. I wouldn't say I was a complete perfectionist, I just liked to give my all to the project at hand. I never quit once I started something; quitting was never an option.

Shadrek called my father Nkosi, which meant King, and my mother Nkozikazi, translated as Queen. He taught me how to get an old fuse to work again by attaching a small piece of copper wire to it. Because we never had a lot of money things had to keep going way past their use by date. I remember so clearly the smell of oil and dust in the workshop. Shadrek did an awful lot of welding. Probably trying to keep things going longer. The borehole was always being struck by lightening and Shadrek would have to do what he could to get it up and running again.

In one of the garages was an old Fiat Topolino. My father had picked it up in an auction somewhere and said it was for me when I was old enough to drive. It was red and convertible. It never did run, but I would often play around in it, clean it and imagine what fun I would have driving it. He loved old cars. We had a beautiful Morris Minor Traveller station wagon that I learnt to drive in.

All the staff seemed to have countless children. Many of them were my friends. They couldn't speak much English and I couldn't speak Shona, but it never seemed to matter. Bare foot, dressed in rags, the little African children always appeared as happy as could be. They called me Palenda. They would appear outside the kitchen door grinning from ear to ear and say to Mackenzie, the cook, that they wanted to see Miss Palenda. I would go outside to meet them and they would chat away in Shona, giggling and smiling. Mackenzie was a grumpy little man with a moustache. I was a bit nervous of him. He ruled the kitchen with an iron fist and I wasn't allowed to take part in the cooking. Not that it bothered me as I was always happier outdoors anyway.

I would make fishing nets out of old mosquito nets — sometimes not old, sometimes I took new ones and hoped no one would notice — and head to the river. Mud and tadpoles made up the bulk of the experience. Some of the tadpoles we kept, carried home in a bag of water. I would keep them in my bedroom in a bowl and watch them grow.

When they were almost frogs they would be transferred into the fishpond that my father had built for my sister, Vicky and me, in the garden. It was below my bedroom window and of course the tadpoles grew into frogs that croaked at dawn in varying tones and intensities that would wake the heaviest of sleepers. One day I could take it no longer and I collected as many of them as I could and took them back to the river, which was not far from the house. The next morning they were back with a vengeance. I didn't bother trying again.

On the other side of the garden my father had built a low stone wall with a small silver gate. It was the entrance to my little garden. My secret garden. In the centre was a beautiful Flamboyant tree. Along the three sides were flower beds. As I mentioned in a previous chapter pansies were my favourite flowers, and they grew in abundance there. To this day I can take myself back to smell of the earth, to the peace and tranquillity of that space. I did as much of the gardening as I could myself, aided when required by the oh so creative Freddy. Freddy would meet me there in the afternoons between 3 and 4.30 pm. Equipped with a budza and shovel he would listen intently to my vision for the garden. A budza was similar to a hoe. Sometimes I drew my ideas on paper. I was creating a masterpiece behind that little wall. Patient and kind, Freddy completed the hard work leaving me with the job of planting. Sometimes I would visit the garden in the mornings to find that Freddy had come in during his own time and continued the work as a surprise for me.

When I was ten, a group of African children arrived at the door with a cardboard box. 'For madam Palenda,' they said. I opened the box and inside was a baby owl. Africans are superstitious about owls. Owls and chameleons. This little bundle was lucky it hadn't been killed. I wasn't sure at that stage what kind of owl it was because it was still fluffy. Thrilled to bits, I nurtured my new pet and as it grew I was able to identify it as an eagle owl. An aviary was built for it outside the kitchen because I was nervous about releasing it into the wild in case it couldn't fend for itself. I loved that owl and was devastated when a dog dug into the aviary one night and killed it.

CHAPTER THIRTEEN
Darker days

"All that's left will be your bones. No flesh, no warmth, nothing to love, and still these dreaded souls will say 'still not thin enough.'
A.W

When I think back to my time at the day-school, Digglefold I can remember imagining it would be like Enid Blyton's Mallory Towers. But, I was trapped in my own inner world; a bubble that wouldn't let anyone else in. I wanted to make friends so much but I knew they didn't want to be my friends because I appeared so different to them. I never went to parties, and I had no idea what the latest fashions were. I guess I must have looked like a nerd to them, but it was very different from my side, and when I watched them laughing and sharing jokes and stories I felt so left out that I truly believed there must be something wrong with me. Why couldn't I express myself? Why couldn't I play? Why was I always the little girl sitting alone on the bench that no one wanted to be near?

I blamed my parents; wished they were younger, wished they had friends with children of my own age. I often thought that if they had a better car perhaps the other children would like me; the illogical reasoning of an unhappy, insecure child. Oddly, though, I never had any issue with adults. I was used to the role I'd been taught to play with them: be polite, speak only when spoken to and remember your manners. Easy; it didn't get any harder than that. Until, the school camp.

Our camp leader was a young man of about twenty-six. The camp was being held at a game park and on one of the days we got to ride ponies; for me this was heaven. Finally, I would have a chance to show the other children that I wasn't useless. The camp leader was tough and he ran it like a military operation. Unfortunately, every time he asked another child how to ride or sort the ponies tack I interrupted to tell everyone what I knew, because I knew that I knew more than he did. But, he didn't like this one bit and told me to shut up, no one was interested in what I had to say. I was crushed. It had taken a lot of courage for me to speak up, and my one attempt at trying to be a valued part of the group had been dashed to pieces.

Isolated and emotionally battered, I buried myself in my work. Fortunately, I loved studying. I was good at it, just for a change, and I got excellent grades. The great thing about being at day-school was that I went home every day, and as soon as I reached Melfort, I felt safe. It was as though I had a personality change. I lit up, ran to my ponies and felt complete. It was always that way. Melfort was the only place where I felt connected to myself, and it had nothing to do with my parents.

I have such fond memories of the winter evenings after school. I would run straight into the kitchen, grab a piece of delicious sponge cake cooked by Joe who was our cook at that time, then sit in front of the roaring fire in the hall.

When I reached Grade 12 it was compulsory to become a weekly boarder. Once again the trunk was packed; a bigger trunk this time. I had outgrown thoughts of Paddington Bear and Mallory's Towers by this time; I knew I had to see this through to the end.

It was all right at first. I missed home but the weekends came round fairly fast. Then, about two months into the first term the bullying began. There were two girls that did it; always the same two girls. They pushed me over in the corridors, stopped me from getting into the dormitory, laughed at me and called me useless. I felt tormented and afraid. The more they bullied me the worse I felt, and the more I started to hate myself. I was too afraid to tell anyone.

Then, they said I was fat. This ate away at me, a burning pain that festered and grew. Night after night I cried myself to sleep. The pressure mounted inside me with nowhere to go. Like a hunted animal trapped in a corner, I could either be killed or fight back. I made a secret plan and chose to fight back. Never again, would anyone call me fat.

I didn't love myself, I hated my body, hated how useless I felt socially. Having my secret plan gave me something to help me numb the pain. I began by cutting down on food portions. After a few weeks I had lost enough weight to notice it. No one else did. I skipped my breaks, avoided desserts and started leaving food. It meant that I would then have to clear the table because whoever finished last at boarding school had that job, but I didn't care.

At home, I would fill my bowl with something bulky like lettuce first, then place whatever we were eating on top of it so it looked like I was eating a lot. I would also eat slowly, then throw my food out of the window when the rest of the family had left the room. I would go in for breakfast early, put crumbs on my plate and say I'd already eaten.

My clothes got looser so I took them in. I would wear baggy clothing at home and my jumper at school. I would shower away from the other girls and at home made sure my mother never saw me naked.

I began to welcome the hunger pangs. They gave me something to focus on, distracting me from how unhappy I was. Finally, I thought I had some sort of control over my life. I was no longer a victim. I don't remember having issues with energy. That might have been due to high levels of the stress hormone cortisol. I must have been highly stressed most of the time.

It's only now, when I look back, that I realise how deep seated the emotions were that I'd been carrying from a very young age. Only now can I understand why I did this. Why I chose and welcomed self abuse. It's amazing what ends one will go to when one has no self worth at all and the guilt is simply too heavy to bear.

The amazing thing was that no one noticed — for months and months.

Eventually my mother did. One day she came into my room when I was changing and was horrified to see how emaciated

I'd become. She contacted the school immediately who, needless to say, claimed to know nothing about it.

I was removed from that school and taken to the doctor. He referred me to a child psychologist. Many an hour was spent sitting in a cold, quiet room being asked questions: "how do you feel?" "why did you do it?" I was too shut down. How could I open up to a stranger, when I couldn't even open up to myself. It became very clear that wasn't going to work. A friend of my mother's suggested taking me to see a homeopath for an alternative approach. I was taken to see Del Smith in Harare.

She worked from home, and I felt instantly comfortable with her. The treatment room was full of books; masses of natural healing books. Del used a pendulum as part of her diagnostic techniques. She would swing it over various little bottles while asking me questions, questions the psychologist had never asked. I told her things I hadn't told anyone. I told her about my crippling shyness, my inability to express myself and my fear of being judged. I told her how useless I felt; how I had been bullied and trapped. I remember she accepted everything I said with no judgement whatsoever.

She gave me an assortment of packets containing tiny, little, white pills. On each packet she had written instructions and also what it was for. I must say I was sceptical. I really didn't believe that those little pills were going to make me better. I took them though; religiously over a three-month period and I did feel a bit better. I still wouldn't eat much but I wasn't actively starving myself anymore. I still saw a fat person in the mirror, but I had stopped losing weight.

I don't know if it was the homeopathics, all I know is that the combination of those and leaving boarding school achieved a marked improvement, and I was able to begin to function 'normally' again.

I put inverted commas around 'normally' because it was many years before I saw myself as healthy. I revisited this place a few more times before letting it go completely, and I will write of that later.

The homeopathic treatment also sparked an interest in natural healing and herbal medicine that I would investigate further in later years.

****

CHAPTER FOURTEEN
My father's death

"Unexpressed emotions will never die, they are buried alive and will come forth later in uglier ways."
Sigmund Freud

While I was recovering from the anorexia my father was diagnosed with prostrate cancer.

He began a series of radiation treatments in the UK and before he left for the first set he asked me to take care of my mother and sister, and I promised I would. He assured us he would be healthy again soon, and the family would return to normal. I knew no matter what happened I couldn't let him down; I had to be the strong one.

Every time he returned he seemed a little weaker, a little thinner. In December 1991, he made his last trip and was home for Christmas. Three of my five half brothers came over from the UK to share that Christmas with us and to help my father with the farm. Looking back perhaps they knew how ill he really was. I didn't.

My thirteenth birthday came and went. I was a teenager now.

My father's health continued to deteriorate. Further tests revealed the cancer had spread to his bones. There was nothing that could be done to help him. During the next few months a nightmare of agony and sadness ensued; he was in terrible pain. One day he was sitting on the swing sofa in the area we called Daddy's Garden, quite close to my little garden, which was full of my father's favourite roses. I had come out to see him, followed by a posse of dogs and one of them brushed against his legs. He yowled in pain and the tears in his eyes nearly broke my heart. I had never seen my father cry before and I felt utterly helpless. Not long after this incident he became bedridden.

Andrew was still living in the swimming pool cottage and drinking more than ever. He was drunk most days from early in the morning. He would come over to our house for morning tea, to see how my father was getting on. For some reason, probably the effects of alcohol in his brain, he became convinced that evil forces were at play in our home and that spells had been cast upon us. He convinced my mother of this, and then offered to bring in witch doctors to heal him and rid the house of evil.

Witch doctors, or N'angas as they're called in the Shona tribe of Zimbabwe are traditional healers that rid people of evil spells. The Africans are in awe of them and take what they say very seriously. As I write, the anxiety I felt all those years ago wells up. I watched from a distance. They were dressed in cow skins and wore hideous wooden masks. There was a band of white around the eye piece which was meant to give them the ability to see illness and evil. There were three of them, plus a few followers to observe.

They were taken to my father's bedroom. They stood over him, and began calling on their spirit guides. Terrifying sounds came out of them as they apparently drew the curse and the illness out of his body. They insisted that spells had been cast upon him and from under his bed appeared to produce the tail of a rabbit as proof.

Once the 'evil' had been removed they made a procession through the rest of the house placing small plastic bottles of salt water in strategic places to ward off further witchcraft.

Looking back at it, I see it like a scene from a horror movie. I knew at the time it was wrong, very wrong. It was a violation of my father's privacy and his beliefs as a Christian. It was like an evil invasion and the bitter smells of their visit lingered for days. I was furious and begged for it never to happen again. But I was never listened to, and they came back to invade our home once more.

I sat on my father's bed as he slept and, sobbing, I apologised. Although it hadn't been my doing I was devastated that he'd been subjected to it. I held his cold, pale hand and cried. I knew what he needed was the love of his family, respect and prayer, not this abomination. I was angry and afraid. The most important person in my life was slipping away and I couldn't stop it.

Mrs Mahomad was next. She was an elderly woman who lived in one of the cottages on the farm. I sensed that she'd had a very hard life. She spoke with a slight lisp and resembled a gypsy with her long grey hair. She claimed to be able to see things: visions and spirits.

Once more my poor father was put through the wringer.

She rubbed heat rub on his legs; the most painful part of his body and even today I can't stand the smell of it. It permeated the house and clung to the air like stale fish.

I was finding life harder and harder to bear. I would hide in my room away from people as much as I could. I didn't know what to believe. Every morning and every night my mother, my sister and I would come together in prayer. My mother told us that the Lord said: "when two or three are gathered in my name I will grant their request." Daddy was going to be healed. Yet deep inside I knew he wasn't. I didn't want to know and I tried to believe otherwise because I couldn't conceive of life without my father. It was like living in a nightmare and not being able to wake up.

My father was soon unrecognisable; pitifully thin, just skin and bone, sheet-white and barely able to move. He said very little and slept most of the time. On good days he would come downstairs and sit in the drawing room which was his favourite room. I wanted to see him, I wanted to be near him, yet I couldn't because it was just too painful.

The alternative methods of healing continued. Another friend had researched the benefits of Vitamin B17 in treating cancer. Apricot kernels contain this in high levels and my poor father was fed these in large amounts. He hated them, but he ate them.

He wasn't improving, and through another friend my mother heard about a healing group that spoke in tongues. She contacted the lady that lead the group and arranged for them to come and pray over my father.

When they arrived they were taken to the drawing room as Daddy had come down stairs that day. They stood over him and began speaking. Weird sounds came from their lips; unlike anything I'd ever heard before. It sounded demonic to me, like something out of a horror film. My intuition told me they were not authentic. I sensed something was wrong.

At the end of the session I entered the drawing room. My father was asleep and when they saw me they told my mother she must beware, for they had seen the devil in my eyes. They told my mother to bring me into the room so they could pray over me and heal me too. I fled. I ran and ran. I curled up in a ball in a paddock about two kilometres from the house and cried till I could I could cry no more. I stayed there until I saw their car drive down the road and turn out onto the main road to Harare.

I hated my mother that day. Hated how she was subjecting my father to those violations of his faith and dignity. But, I'd learnt many years before to keep my mouth shut so I bottled it up as usual. Abject helplessness and despair coursed through my body day and night. I tried to pray. I tried to connect to that peaceful place within me that had always been there, but my emotions were so raw I simply couldn't find it.

At the end of March my father was put onto morphine. He was totally bedridden by this stage and in constant pain. A nurse from Island Hospice would come and see him every week and she recommended that my mother increased the dose. Even though she didn't trust the nurse one bit, she did what was suggested. Shortly after that my father became even less responsive and soon after he developed a respiratory infection.

It was late at night on 17th April when the phone call came. Mother answered it. My sister and I were standing at the top of the stairs leaning over the banisters. She let the phone fall to the floor and wailed. "He's dead! Your daddy is dead." I screamed before falling to my knees in a crumpled mess, wailing uncontrollably. Vicky stood stock still; shocked. She was only eight years old and had no idea how to process this terrible loss. I spent the night in my mother's room, but Vicky stayed in hers. Bewildered, it was days before she could come to terms with what had happened. On the day our father died Vicky had wanted to go to the hospital with me and mother to see him, but instead she'd gone to a horse show. Mother had wanted her to continue her normal activities. Her young mind struggled to come to terms with not being able to say goodbye.

On 22nd April my father was buried on Melfort, as he would have wanted. The service was held at the little church and the burial was at the bottom of one of the side gardens. I remember so little about that day, except for when the pipe band played 'The Last Post' at his graveside and my mother, Vicky and I each dropped a red rose onto his coffin. That was the moment the silent tears began to fall. I turned away, the pain was too much to bear. As I did so I became aware of the large number of Africans who were standing some distance from us. Silently they stood, heads bowed for the man they'd come to respect and the family that remained.

Some of my half brothers had come over for the funeral and they stayed on for a few days before returning the UK.

The rest of the day was a blur, the sympathies from friends fell on deaf ears. I remember my half brother Paul found me curled up on a couch outside on the veranda. He said we'd be OK.

A beautiful headstone was built out of rocks from the river at Melfort, and the poem he'd asked for was written in the cement. We planted roses. He loved roses.

It's only now, as I write this, that I realise I never healed from his death. I packaged up the emotion and pain in a box and hid it deep inside me. I grew up in just a few days. I had to, or at least I thought I had to. None of us processed his death – there was no grieving period and looking back I now see how the three of us just shut it out. My mother didn't cope well and needed help with the running of the farm. She needed someone strong to talk to and that was me. Vicky needed a role model, a sister she could look up to. She'd always been a very brave person and during those times showed little emotion. Like me, she was raised to be a 'soldier's daughter' and never cry. I remember the lost, confused look in her eyes. How painful it must have been for her. I wanted so much to be everything to both of them, yet I had so little to give. All I really wanted to do was run away.

I never talked to anyone about his death, about how I felt or how I dealt with it. Or in fact, didn't deal with it. Even in my work with counsellors and life coaches in years to come I kept this locked very firmly away.

I also did something else. I turned my back on my faith. I closed my heart off from the world and set the core belief that it wasn't safe to love because whatever I loved would be taken away from me.

I reinforced the belief that life was cruel and out to get me. I cursed God for what he'd done and then believed I would forever be made to suffer for my curse. I didn't care at that point; I'd suffered so much already I'd come to believe it was my due. I believed I must be a bad person who deserved to be punished.

I didn't even realise I held these beliefs until now. I've spent years holding this inside me, I hardly processed his passing at all, just buried it and kept going.

So many times I would go to his graveside and talk to him, cry for him. Ask him why. Why he had left us and how on earth were we going to survive without him. I had no idea how to process such an awful loss. There was no one to talk to, no one at all. I saw him everywhere, there was no escape. Part of me died when he died, and it's only now as I gently nurture myself through the process of writing about my loss that I can feel that part of me slowly open and breathe again. Like cold concrete, that part of my heart lay stiff and lifeless, surrounded by thorns. I cry now as I cried then, only now I'm older and decades have passed. Now I'm not afraid to let myself heal for I know I will be OK. I am OK.

For a long time, my mother was unable to accept he was gone. I feebly tried to deal with my own grief yet I felt her pain too. She was lost, she was afraid and she had no one to turn to. Even though I was still angry with her I knew she needed me. And, I loved her.

I remembered my beloved father's words: "Take care of your mother and your sister." I had to shut the pain away. I had to be a soldier's daughter. I had to grow up. And grow up I did. Life was never the same again.

My childhood ended with my father's passing. I took on the role of family supporter and helped my mother with the day to day running of the farm. She turned to me for monetary advice, help with business decisions and emotional support. Vicky seemed to be OK. I often thought it was because of the fact that she'd always been closer to our mother than our father.

I was thirteen. I did the best I could, but the pressure was unbearable. Every day I would sit with her and do the daily accounts. I didn't really understand it and I found it painful to do as it reminded me so much of my father. She would ask me how we were going to survive. I didn't know, but I did my best to reassure her we would.

It didn't really bring us any closer though, my mother and I. We had to work together to survive but there was always that barrier; that deep seated fear in me of upsetting her. I had learnt so early on what to do and say to be what she wanted, I'd lost the ability to let her see the real me. I think after father's death the real me was truly forgotten. I felt I had lost my life in a way too and that I would forever be obliged to fulfil my promise.

Four months after his death a neighbour asked if I wanted to go with her to polocrosse practice. It was played every Sunday at the local country club, Ruwa. My mother said I could go so off I went one Sunday with my pony.

Polocrosse is a combination of lacrosse and polo. It's known as 'poor man's polo' as you don't need to have several ponies like you do in polo. It's played in a team of three. The game originated in Australia in 1935 and has been labelled: King of the One Horse Sports. It is acknowledged as one of only three truly Australian sports, the other two being Australian Rules Football and Camp Drafting.

I was lent a stick and ball and shown the basic concepts of the game. I was hooked straight away, it was so much more fun than Showing and Dressage, and there was none of the snobbery that I'd hated. For the first time since my father's death I felt like I was having some fun and it got me away from the pressures of having to run the farm. Fortunately, my pony was very quiet and didn't seem to mind me wielding a stick on his back!

Soon I was going every week and it wasn't long before I needed a proper polocrosse pony that could stop on a dime and turn fast. Through a friend at the club mother bought me an elderly thoroughbred mare named Diane. She had a stubborn streak but I understood her and we made a brilliant team. In between practices I would work on my ball skills. I was always a very determined child and liked to be proficient in everything I did. Every afternoon I would head out to the riding school with my stick and ball and practice for an hour or so. It was good for me to have something else to focus on, and with each session I got better and better.

****

CHAPTER FIFTEEN
Alcoholism

"Addiction is a monster, it lives inside and feeds off you, takes from you, controls you and destroys you. It is a beast that tears you apart, rips out your soul, and laughs at your weakness."
Anonymous

One day, we were in the clubhouse at the polocrosse club after practice having some lunch when one of the adults offered me a drink. In those days there were no age limits for drinking in Zimbabwe, and I also looked older than I was so perhaps, in fairness, the adult in question hadn't realised I was only fourteen.

It was vodka and coke. I remember quite clearly how I felt after that first drink. I felt lighter, chattier, happier and freer from the emotional pain I'd been carrying around for days on end. Freer from the responsibilities that weighed upon my young shoulders. It was amazing. I was able to talk to people without the excruciating shyness that normally plagued me.

I began to look forward to my weekly drink after practice. Then, I asked my mother if I could have some wine with her during our evening meal. My parents had never believed in restricting us so naturally she said yes. Looking back, it was probably quite nice for her to have someone to share that with.

But, I drank to get away from myself and quickly developed a tolerance for it, thereby needing more and more to get the same effect.

Polocrosse was a huge sport in Zimbabwe and every fortnight large tournaments were held where teams from around the country would compete against each other. As soon as I was a good enough player I was put in a team and started taking part. They were very social events. Each club held one and the team would often travel for several hours to attend. We would travel down on the Friday and set up our campsite in the afternoon. The horses would be trucked down. I had a groom called Shadrek who was an alcoholic. He would drink for most of the Friday and Saturday nights and would often still be drunk when he prepared my pony for the 8 am game in the morning. My game was always the first of the day because I was in the lowly 'C' division —the bottom one! How I never fell off a badly cinched saddle I don't know!

I was very competitive and loved being part of the team; I played mostly with adults because there were very few teenagers in the club. They were a carefree bunch. Kind and easy going. I always felt looked after by them.

It was not long before I outgrew my pony Diane, so my mother bought me new ones. First, there was King's Venture, a thoroughbred horse off the track. She'd won a race and then burnt out. She was placed in the thoroughbred sales and a polocrosse player who trained and sold ponies bought her. After three months of intensive training she was put on the market. The poor thing literally didn't know what'd hit her.

After being trained to race in a straight line she now had to stop and turn on a dime. She had no brakes and was constantly stressed, but we quickly developed a bond and I spent months hacking her out in between games so she learnt to relax. Brakes were a bit of an issue, but I managed. There was the odd occasion that I would be seen flying over the line at the end of the field, going full tilt towards the fence. Fortunately, we never have an accident.

Once she had calmed down and I knew her really well I would often let her gallop as fast as she wanted on the farm. There was a long stretch of road in the paddock we called Dam Paddock and this was a favourite sprinting track. There's something exhilarating about galloping flat out on a horse, so fast that the tears flow down your cheeks. I was never afraid; I knew Venture would look after me.

Not long after we had Venture mother bought me Season's Wonder. My mother loved to go to the thoroughbred winter sales because you could pick up horses very cheaply. She would then turn them into brood mares. On this particular occasion I went with her and fell in love with the beautiful, dark, eight-year-old bay mare the instant I saw her. She had huge kind eyes and a gentle nature. I trained her for polocrosse myself. I'm sure she must have wondered what on earth was going on when she was being taught to stop, turn and gallop on command. At the end of my second season with her we won Best Number 3 at my club. I was very proud of us both; she was the gift that kept on giving.

Unfortunately, with the tournaments came more drinking. There was always a disco on the Saturday night and all the members of the different clubs would get together. Desperate to fit in, to not appear weird and shy I would drink. I would drink from early in the evening and continue until late into the night. To begin with everything seemed fine. I would happily dance, chat to everyone and have a wonderful time. No one seemed to think there was a problem.

But after a while, the people I would chat to at night began chatting to me during the day when I was sober, when I was back to my incredibly shy self. I didn't know what to do, so I nipped at the odd drink during the day as well. I must've been about fifteen by then. Because I was developing a tolerance for it I had no trouble playing the sport after drinking so it naturally led to more and more.

Then came the blackouts. I was horrified the first time it happened. A friend of mine had escorted me back to my tent in the wee hours and I'd woken in the morning with no recollection whatsoever of what'd happened. But it wasn't enough to stop me. The addiction had me in its thrall by this stage.

At the same time as the polocrosse and the drinking, I was doing a correspondence course at home to complete my 'O' levels. My mother had found me a tutor who was based in Marondera, a small town about an hour away. Her name was Mrs Smith and she became a stabilising influence in my life. Vicky and I both went to her, along with three other girls of similar ages. My most difficult subject was maths and that was Mrs Smith's strong point.

Mrs Smith had grown up in a very poor family in England. She would tell us about the nights she spent studying by candle light to pass her exams. She was a very intelligent lady. She and her husband had moved to Zimbabwe when it was still called Rhodesia in the 1970s to work as missionaries.

The Smiths had two Chow Chows. As I had grown up with just about every breed of dog you could imagine it was interesting to see these; they had blue tongues and the loveliest of natures.

I continued to drink at tournaments but kept it together during the week; I have Mrs Smith to thank for that. She would spend hours helping me with my studies and really drove home the importance of getting a good education.

At the end of 1995, I completed my 'O' levels and much to my delight came out with great results. Mrs Smith had worked her magic and I was now free to take a break before 'A' levels began.

****

CHAPTER SIXTEEN
Granny's death

"Grandmas hold our tiny hands for just a little while, but our hearts forever."
Anon

Towards the end of 1995 my dearest granny became ill in England. It all seemed to happen very quickly and by the end of the year she had passed away. It was very hard losing yet another person I loved. No one is ever ready to lose a loved one but I think losing her only four years after my father was too hard. My mother, Vicky and I went over for her funeral. I was very aware of the guilt my mother was feeling because she hadn't been there when granny passed. There was also so much that was unhealed in their relationship, and my poor mother struggled. She didn't talk about it much, but I could feel it. I wished I could've helped her.

Granny was buried in Selborne as she'd requested and the ceremony was beautiful. She had embroidered four footstool covers for the church before she died and they were set in place in time for her funeral.

It was winter, and we stood in the cold after the service to pay our last respects. That was the year I saw snow for the first time. We stayed at The Queen's hotel where we'd always stayed before and the owner, Mr. Paton, was very kind. The whole village loved my granny and came to see her off that day.

My mother didn't know what to do with Granny's cottage, but she wanted to have it dealt with quickly. Before we returned to Melfort she arranged for all of Granny's belongings to be shipped to us. The cottage was to be sold.

Back in Zimbabwe, it was hauntingly surreal having to unpack Granny's life. All her treasures, her art equipment, sketches, pencils, even the eraser she'd used. But Melfort was huge so, of course, we found places for everything.

****

CHAPTER SEVENTEEN
Dance of the heart then back to school

"Falling in love is like the rain. You can't predict it, but you can always see signs of it before it completely falls."
Anon

Three months after Granny died life threw me something wondrous: I fell in love. Like clouds that part to reveal a clear blue sky, the darkness of losing my granny lifted to allow a new bloom.

A friend of Granny's contacted us and asked if her grandson could stay with us for a while as he was travelling to Zimbabwe for three months during his gap year. We collected him from the airport and took him to Melfort.

It became apparent very quickly that we liked each other. I'd never had a boyfriend before so it was very new and exciting. For a few precious weeks I was unbelievably happy. I travelled with him to unfamiliar parts of Zimbabwe, and saw life through completely different eyes, laughing like never before.

We went on a canoeing safari along the Zambezi river; all the way to Mana Pools from Kariba Dam. Mana Pools is a wildlife conservation area in Northern Zimbabwe. It was wonderful. Our days were spent paddling down river under the hot African sun, on the watch for crocodiles on the banks and avoiding pods of hippos in the water. At night we would set up tents and sit around a campfire. I hadn't realised that when hippos talk to each other it sounds like a hearty chortle.

We also visited the magnificent Victoria Falls and went white water rafting. I couldn't believe how much I'd never seen of the beautiful country I lived in. But it couldn't last forever and after three months he returned to England. I was heartbroken. We wrote to each other for a while, but that soon faded; we were very young. It was a passing light and I treasured the memories. Something I have always regretted was not telling him how I felt. I didn't know how to, and so I said nothing, but I wish I'd been able to. Not because it would have changed anything, but just so he could have known what a bright light he'd shed on my world.

After he left I talked to my mother about 'A' levels, and we decided I should return to school. So, in June 1996, I started at Watershed College.

I gave up polocrosse that year too. I needed to focus on my studies and it kept me away from alcohol; mostly. I took English literature, Art and Biology. English literature was my favourite subject. I would spend countless hours working on my essays; to lose myself in the world of language was comforting, and I wrote poetry, short stories and articles for the local paper.

Writing had always been something that had captured my mind. It's amazing how pictures can be painted through words. You can take your reader on exciting adventures, weave a trail that ignites curiosity and stirs emotions. Worlds open up; dimensions never known or imagined before. Time stands still when I write and I can plug in to mysterious territories that lure me in. I digress, let me return to my school days.

I seemed to be getting my life back on track. I still struggled to make friends, but by now I'd accepted that. I didn't socialise much and I was still quite isolated, but at least it was more positive.

I wanted to be a journalist and an author. To me the thought of being able to write every single day for the rest of my life and get paid for it, was heavenly. Plus, I wanted to help others and journalism seemed to be a perfect way to do it.

I had two English literature teachers, one of whom was Mr Davidson. I used to talk to him a lot about my writing. He was immensely supportive and when I told him I wanted to write a book he said, "Do it." I'd been horrified by the genocide in Rwanda and had read about it in the papers a few years before, and I was drawn to write about it. He encouraged me to do so, but I never did. Many years later I read the book, *'Left to Tell,'* by Imacul`ee Ilibigiza and I thought of my unwritten work. *'Left to Tell,'* is the harrowing story of a young woman's journey during the genocide; how she discovered unconditional love and forgave her family's killers.

In 1997, I left school with three 'A' levels and a dream. I was going to university in England to study English Literature and

Philosophy. Then, I was going to join the United Nations. I had huge dreams of helping the world; of being of service to others. Yet, I had this gnawing sense of guilt that still plagued me. I felt guilty leaving my family, as though I was obliged to stay and look after them.

It's funny writing this now and connecting to the person I was back then. Even though there had been so much pain, I still wanted to give; the two things are not mutually exclusive.

Around the same time, I developed a strong interest in spirituality. Having shut any form of faith out after my father died it was comforting to explore something deeper. But I still held on to a lot of heartache I hadn't even begun to release. I had no idea how to, and was too scared. I read a lot of books by Paramahansa Yogananda, an Indian Yogi and Guru. It was because of these that I started meditation, and I practiced daily. I also found Wayne Dyer's, *'The Awakened Life.'* One of my half brothers had given it to my father many years earlier and it'd been sitting at the back of a cupboard for years. I was absolutely inspired by him.

I explored my love of writing and painting. I painted from imagination, images and patterns inspired from my spiritual readings. Looking back, it was a positive time for me.

The response from my university applications came back, and to my delight I'd been accepted for Queens University, Belfast. My mother had studied in Belfast and although I'd never been there I felt a connection to the place.

But life had other plans in store for me and before I even responded to the universities, I was diverted yet again.

****

CHAPTER EIGHTEEN
Rose tinted glasses

"Don't put the key to your happiness in someone else's pocket."
Anon

I started going to polocrosse tournaments again, not as a player, but as a supporter and it wasn't long before I was drinking heavily once more. Still suffering from acute shyness and lack of social skills the alcohol took hold as my familiar crutch. I made friends with a young woman called Debbie who was about six years older than me. She hardly drank at all but we still became great friends. By this time, I had a car and a driving licence and we would go clubbing in the city centre. We would party every Wednesday, Friday and Saturday, often until dawn. Because I still lived on the farm and wasn't working I had no responsibilities, so quite easily, I slid off the rails. I have a lot to thank Debbie for when I remember how she drove me home on many an occasion.

After a few months of living like that something else developed. On a trip to Marondera I met a young man called J in the supermarket. He was the brother of someone I'd gone to school with. Very soon we were seeing each other regularly and it wasn't long before I was in love, again. J was everything I'd ever wanted in a man. He played rugby, was the life and soul of the party, and was always up to something. He turned my world upside down and I was besotted.

But, my drinking escalated. By this stage I was drinking during the day and hiding bottles of vodka in my bedroom. I had an 'anais anais' backpack hanging on the side of my full length mirror and this was where I kept them. When I stayed with my J I premixed bottles of vodka and juice and hid them in my suitcase. I would get up early in the morning and drink before anyone else was up so that I was chatty and bubbly when they did. I had tunnel vision, all I saw was the next drink, but I was also in love; I'd found the one person that would make me happy.

The amazing thing was J never seemed to notice. I think because our time together always involved parties and drinking anyway, I somehow got away with it.

But at the level of about a bottle of vodka a day, there comes the point when the body and mind has had enough. The blackouts grew worse; they were part of everyday life. And then there were the vicious mood swings. They scared me the most. I would yell and accuse J of all sorts of things when in that state.

Yet I carried on. I carried on killing myself slowly and driving the people that loved me further and further away, and I had no obvious way of stopping it. I was caught in a noose that was tightening around my neck and I couldn't even utter a peep. I could see my family judging me. I hated myself yet had nowhere to turn? I couldn't admit I had a drinking problem because if I did I'd have to stop, and if I stopped the man I loved would see how empty and shy I was, and would leave me.

My world became very dark. Terrified of losing J I became paranoid. I questioned his every move. I wove a web of fear and mistrust into every situation.

Drug addiction is something that cannot be understood by someone who hasn't experienced it. They can try and imagine, but never know the full extent. It steals your soul, turns you into something you don't recognise — and don't want to — but it refuses to release you until there's nothing left.

Self respect, self worth, self love — these terms mean nothing when you're caught in the whirlpool of addiction. Survival is all you know. It consumes you, you can feel its teeth ripping into your flesh, but there's no escape. You scream a scream that no one can hear.

I loathed the person I'd become. I was so far from who I'd been I didn't see how recovery was possible. I didn't see anything except the next drink.

Eventually J mentioned it and said he knew. My mother had told him because she was worried about me. He said he would help me out of the darkness, and I knew I had to try.

Slowly, one day at a time, I clawed my way out of the pits of hell. I had the shakes daily, I hallucinated, I couldn't sleep; it was horrendous. What was even worse was that as my mind began to clear I remembered some of things I'd done when I was drunk and I felt unbearably humiliated and ashamed. I hadn't grown up this way. I was a good person; how had I ended up like that? My family didn't know me anymore and probably didn't want to. We were only a small family — just the three of us. How could I have done this to them, or myself?

After about six months, life improved and J asked me to marry him. He gave me a beautiful ring and I was blissfully happy; I was going to marry my best friend.

I look back and see how crazy it was. Best friend? I didn't know who I was let alone who he was, or what a best friend was. Yet we stayed engaged. There was one period where it was broken off, but it didn't last long. At the time, I thought I was happy, but now I see I was in a dream world.

We moved in to one of the houses on the farm. It was called Landsdowne. It was a beautiful bungalow with a huge garden that included a swimming pool. I swam daily. Our wedding had been set for September 2000 and I wanted to be in shape. I was obsessed with losing weight and got upset if I missed a day of swimming. I didn't realise at the time that I was still harbouring remnants of anorexia. I saw little of my mother or sister at that time. I don't think they knew how to take me. I was a ghost of the person they'd known.

Every Sunday we had a braai and all J's friends were invited. Those were happy occasions. I felt a sense of purpose preparing food for the lunch and being the hostess. J and I agreed that as I appeared to be much better it would be fine to have the occasional drink for a special occasion. It was fine, for a while. But the root of the problem was still there. The anguish had never been processed and released. So one drink inevitably led to another. And another. The vicious cycle began again. Every time we had an argument, every time my inner bubble felt prodded, I would drink the fear away. If only I'd been able to stay away from it, we might have been all right. But I couldn't.

And, as if that was not enough, more trauma was on its way.

****

CHAPTER NINETEEN
The end of an era

"Never seek the wind in the field – it is useless to try and find what is gone."
Old Polish Proverb

If anyone had asked me in 1996 where I would be living for the rest of my life, I would have said Zimbabwe. Never in my wildest dreams could I have envisioned what the following few years would bring. In order to have some sort of understanding of how the troubles started I have included a brief history of land reform and the subsequent crisis.

In 1979, the Lancaster House agreement was signed ending white rule in Zimbabwe. The Land Apportionment Act of 1930, which had promoted unjust division of land, was abolished and Britain agreed to fund reform on a 'willing buyer, willing seller' basis. This was to be in place for ten years.

The Land Acquisition Act of 1985 enabled the government to have first option to purchase excess land with the 'willing buyer, willing seller' basis still in place. This had limited impact due to the government having insufficient funds to reimburse land owners. In 1995, that clause was removed from the Land Acquisition Act enabling the government to purchase land on a compulsory basis, and pay compensation.

This year also saw the withdrawal of aid to the land reform programme by the British.

In 1996, veterans of the liberation war saw their payments from the War Victims Compensation Fund suspended. This led, understandably, to conflict. They took to the streets the following year demanding gratuities, pensions, and land in a national strike that paralysed the country.

Payments were made, and as a result 14th November, 1997 — commonly known as Black Friday — witnessed the Zimbabwe dollar lose 71.5% value against the US dollar. Shortly after in 1998, food prices rocketed, fuel ran dry and riots crammed the streets. The economic crisis escalated fast.

In 1999, aid to Zimbabwe from the IMF (International Monetary Fund) and the World Bank was suspended owing to disagreements with the government concerning policies.

In February 2000, Mugabe's government lost the referendum on constitutional reforms. Faced with growing opposition his supporters began seizing white-owned farms in what was known as the 'fast track land reform program'. The invaders, supposedly war veterans, were of all ages. Armed with machine guns, axes, batons and whatever they could get their hands on, they went to farms in truck loads and left a trail of trauma and violence. The first wave of invasions saw the seizing of 110,000 square kilometres of land. The farm workers were chased from their farms leaving them unemployed and homeless.

It was horrific. On Saturday 15th April, 2000, the first white farmer was murdered. He was taken from his home into the bush and shot. The five farmers that were trying to help him were also abducted and beaten. The farmer's wife was in town when it happened and fortunately someone contacted her before she returned home with her two-year-old twins, warning her not to go back to the farm.

I saw the photos on the cover of the newspaper and the hairs on the back of my neck stood on end. I felt sick. The nightmare was real.

My mother wouldn't leave the farm. She said nothing would happen to us. I wasn't so sure.

Violence, fear and corruption continued unabated. The police did nothing, there was no law, just mounting tension. Crime exploded in all areas. Inflation shot up and queuing for almost non-existent fuel was part of everyday life.

My wedding took place in September of that same year. In sad and troubled times it had been planned, and in sad and troubled times it was held.

My beautiful dress was handmade by a very talented lady who lived nearby. I had chosen an Elizabethan style, off white with beautiful cream lace and cord; my dream dress. My mother didn't want the wedding to go ahead. She knew I was having issues with alcohol, and what with the stress of the farm invasions and my mental state, she wasn't convinced going through with it was the wisest decision. But my heart was set on it, and I went ahead and did most of the preparations on my own. My friend Debbie helped me. She was my matron of honour and her mother made the cake and did the flowers for the church. My sister, Vicky, was my bridesmaid.

The day before the wedding I collected some beautiful fresh flowers. I can still remember the smell of them in my car. I spent most of the day at Debbie's house and in the afternoon we decorated the church. Upon every aisle we hung a beautiful posy with trailing gypsophila. The cake was exquisite! It had two tiers and each one was the shape of a teardrop.

On the morning of my wedding day I had my hair done. Gypsophila was threaded through the curls. Vicky, my mother and Debbie drank champagne in the drawing room. I never intended to drink very much at all. One of our dearest family friends, Tom English, was to give me away. He drove the wedding party to the church and walked me up the aisle. I remember holding his hand, my cheeks slightly flushed from the champagne. I was in love, still very young, and scared stiff. Ahead of me I saw my husband-to-be looking so incredibly handsome in his suit. I could've cried. Time stood still in that moment. I had arranged a magnificent black horse and carriage to take us to the reception, so after the ceremony we climbed in and were off. But there was already a slight tension. J knew I'd been drinking, and I sensed his disappointment.

The first hour or so of the reception went well; the rest I would rather forget. I had gone past the point of knowing when, or how, to stop drinking, and I slipped into the old familiar routine. I have vague memories of crying, hating myself, and wishing I was dead. My next memory is of being woken at Melfort by J, and being taken home. I was dazed. For days I just wanted to run away. How could I ever forgive myself for what I'd done — fighting and yelling at J for no apparent reason on what was meant to be the happiest day of my life? For running out of the reception in a state of drunken hysteria before locking myself in a room with a glass of brandy in hand and refusing to come out. It wasn't even so much my actions that mortified me, but that I'd let myself get so drunk in the first place. I knew what I was like drunk, unreasonable and volatile.

I think we both believed we'd made a mistake, but neither of us knew what to do about it. I knew I loved him but only in the capacity I was capable of. Life was crazy with the farm invasions and the stress. We both just took it one moment at a time. We went on our honeymoon to a beautiful area called Nyanga, on the Eastern border. Nyanga was a favourite place of mine; I used to go there with my parents as a child. I remember holding his hand during the drive. Guilt seeped through every pore of my body and I truly believed I would never be happy again. I didn't know what to say, even a hundred sorries would have been inadequate. I couldn't go back; I couldn't erase my drunken and embarrassing behaviour. The memories would forever be etched in my mind. We drank a lot on that honeymoon, pretending everything was going to be OK.

In retrospect, I recognise that was the point when I felt obliged to make up for the damage done, so I wrote letters of apology to all the guests. I never talked to anyone about the stifling anguish that choked me like an ever tightening noose.

I retreated into my darkness and never discussed it again. I didn't feel I deserved any sympathy; not worthy of forgiveness. It's only now, fifteen years later, that I cry for me. Not for the guests, not for J, but for the twenty-one-year old girl that I was. The young girl who drank because she was in pain, and believed she wasn't good enough for the love she'd found, who drank because she thought it made her more of what people wanted. The young girl who dreamt of riding away into the distance with her true love and living happily ever after.

I never realised that I'd buried it all so deep I hadn't been able to find it until now. To be able to release it, to see it through different eyes and to forgive myself is remarkable. My heart feels like it has opened like a rose bud reaching towards the sun, soaking up the warm rays of life and living.

We continued to live at Landsdowne. I continued to drink. Hiding bottles and hating myself, locked in depression. We fought bitterly. I remember his words, how they hurt. Yet I was stuck in a vicious cycle I couldn't break. He talked of divorce, I couldn't absorb it. I felt like I had no one but him, yet he resented me. I was a burden and I knew it. I could do nothing right, his anger pierced my heart and terrified me. And I felt it all, as if it were my own. So odd — that was the only thing I hadn't lost — the ability to read other people's feelings.

At the end of the year J and I drove to South Africa for a few days. When we returned the decline of Zimbabwe was more apparent than ever. We knew we had to leave. My sister-in-law Candice, lived in New Zealand and that was where we chose to go.

I remember us sitting by the swimming pool at Melfort planning our move. We would go for a year. Give Zimbabwe time to come right, then return home. We never intended to be gone long. We talked of the jobs we would get. Anything would do. Sheep farms, dairy farms, our imaginations roamed, and in the plans for the future I saw a light at the end of the long, dark tunnel, a light of hope, that perhaps we, as a couple, would be OK. We left Africa for New Zealand in March 2001.

But not before one final shock.

We went away to stay with a friend for the weekend, and I will never forget the return. We drove round the corner and Melfort came into view. There, in our paddock, was a ZANU PF flag. They'd come. I was trembling when we drove up the drive. My mother was still there and surprisingly calm. Apparently we'd been lucky. This group were not as violent as others, and had settled for the top end of the farm, leaving us to remain in the homestead.

But, it was like living on tenterhooks. I couldn't go anywhere near the areas they'd taken. Huts had been built virtually over night and the sound of felling trees rent the air. We didn't know if they would attack us if we ventured too close so we stayed away. Night time was the worst. Insomnia prevailed and the slightest sound woke me.

What tormented me the most was the utter helplessness of the situation. This was my home, and there was nothing I could do. They were the law now; these youths with guns.

We left Landsdowne and moved into a smaller cottage closer to Melfort in preparation for our move to New Zealand. How was I going to leave my family? I'd promised my father I would look after my mother and my sister and now I was going to desert them. Leave them at the mercy of a lawless dictator. But I was married, I was tied, and my husband was leaving.

My mother was devastated and begged me not to go. I drowned the pain, living like a zombie. My relationship with Vicky got worse. I knew she had little respect for me, and I didn't blame her. She'd looked up to me in the past and I'd let her down.

In March 2001, with our lives packed in two suitcases, we boarded a bus to South Africa, and a plane bound for New Zealand.

The day we left I was totally soused. I sat in the passage at Melfort clinging to my black Labrador, Gravy, and bawling my eyes out. I couldn't say goodbye to my family. It was more than a nightmare. Pried away from Gravy, I was carried to the car and soon enough we were on the bus.

When I ponder on how much I drank during those years I wonder how I actually survived. The body is amazingly forgiving. The amount of abuse it can withstand is extraordinary.

****

CHAPTER TWENTY
Across the world

"Monsters are real, ghosts are real too, they live inside us and sometimes they win." Stephen King

We stayed with my husband's family when we arrived in New Zealand. They lived in a small farming town called Ashburton, which was in the county of Canterbury, an hour south of Christchurch on the South Island.

It wasn't easy to get work permits. You had to get a job that was on the skills shortage list and for us the most likely field was dairy farming. It wasn't long before we'd secured positions on a dairy conversion in a small village at the top of the South Island called Tapawera. Our new boss, Darryl, who was living in Ashburton at the time, lent us his truck to take a drive up there to check it out.

At the top of the farm road you could see the land in the valley below. It was beautiful, like something out of a postcard. We looked at each and both knew we wanted to live there.

In May 2001, our dairy jobs began. We were the only staff, and were employed as herd managers. We were very naive, very innocent and totally unprepared for the gruelling work that lay ahead.

As the farm was a conversion there was a lot of fencing to be done before the cows were due to arrive. Neither of us had done much in the way of physical labour, coming as we did from Zimbabwe, where we were accustomed to staff doing that work. Darryl was a hard, tough man who demanded 110% from us, and, winter was approaching.

We would start work at 8 am and continue until dark, with a lunch break, of course. It was freezing. With numb fingers we bent icy-cold wire and hammered in nails. Our clothing, created for the mild Zimbabwean climate, was hardly suitable for this weather. Merino thermals and thick padded coats became a necessity. The first couple of months we stayed positive, but as the coldest winter in twenty years hit us it became very hard. Our house wasn't insulated and firewood was hard to come by. We kept our bed in the lounge and would wake in the morning to ice inside the window panes.

Then, the cows arrived. There were about 500 of them to start with, and they travelled up from Ashburton in huge trucks. The new paddocks weren't quite ready for them so they were driven up to the hills. But these cows had been born and raised on the flat Canterbury Plains — they'd never seen hills before. Over the course of the next few weeks we found many of them dead or dying on the frozen hills. It was tragic. The loss of livestock meant Darryl's stress levels went through the roof and he demanded more and more hours from us.

The cows that had survived were brought to flatter ground in time for calving which began in July. Never in my life have I worked like I worked then. 70 hour weeks, in freezing conditions, I lost so much weight I could see every rib — without any anorexia in sight. It was all a bit of a blur. Neither of us were happy, and I was terribly homesick.

We had every second weekend off and used that time to explore the area. J started playing rugby for the local Tapawera Club and through that we made some connections, but mostly we were very isolated and lonely.

The news about Zimbabwe worried us more every day. The farm invasions continued, as did the bloody murders of white farmers. The local Africans were suffering too as the ruthless dictator continued unabated. The only contact I had with my family was via snail mail as they had no phone during the troubles. I felt depressed, exhausted, and hopeless. Our plan to return home after a year seemed highly unlikely.

Towards the end of the season an unhappy cow kicked me on the wrist and I very swiftly developed carpal tunnel syndrome. As a result, I had to leave my job. I found another on an apple orchard in the Motueka valley. It was much easier work and for a while my spirits rose. My husband left the dairy farm soon after I did and we moved into a small house on the Motueka river bank. It was a beautiful spot, and I started to run regularly up the hills around us.

Happily, I was in touch with my family again, and Vicky and her partner came to New Zealand to work. I was thrilled to have them there, but depression was taking its toll on me and my mental state deteriorated. I was starving myself again as my perspective of my body was warped.

And, I'd started drinking again.

Somehow, in the midst of this energy-sapping behaviour I managed to complete a correspondence course as a fitness instructor. I was desperate to get out of the life I was stuck in.

My marriage wasn't going well. My husband couldn't deal with my depression and we were isolated from my sister and her family who'd settled in Ashburton.

One day I was so desperate I made an appointment to see a doctor who prescribed Aropax. I'm starting to feel nauseous as I write about this, it was one of the most traumatic times of my life. The Aropax helped for a short time, but the depression increased dynamically. I knew my marriage was on the rocks, I had no one to turn to so I began to turn on myself. I hated myself. Hated that I was drinking in secret again; that I was such a burden on my husband. I would often think of my family, knowing I'd failed them completely. I would walk alone along the river bank and tears would flow down my cheeks. I would stare into the beautiful clear water and wish I could just float away and never come back. It was during one of those walks that I began to think seriously about ending my life.

The thoughts intensified. My husband was unhappy, I had deserted my family, let them down, broken the promise I made to my father many years ago. No, I thought to myself, no one will miss me. In fact, I'll be doing them a favour.

I planned it all and I wrote a note. Then, that night I took two packets of pain killers hoping I would never wake up. But, wake up I did — with a terrible stomach ache. I told my husband I was ill and wouldn't be going to work. He left for work and I grabbed a bottle. I was delusional, I tried calling Vicky but there was no reply. Desperation overtook me but then J came home, and he was furious to find me drinking. We had a massive fight in the bedroom and I ran into the bathroom and grabbed a razor blade — the blood flowed down my arms in rivers and I was so relieved; finally, there would be no more pain.

Vague memories of the ambulance linger in my mind. The siren blaring, the nurse saying, "Can you hear me Belinda? Stay with me." I wanted so desperately to slip away, to finally find peace from the demons in my head. I wanted to set my loved ones free from the burden of having me in their life.

I think this is where people greatly misjudge suicide. It's thought to be a very selfish act and while it does leave a trail of pain and devastation it is never intended that way. At least it wasn't in my case. I truly believed I was doing the world a favour. Finding myself in that ambulance, still alive? It just embedded what a failure I was into my psyche even deeper. I couldn't even get that right.

I was taken to Nelson Hospital. Once I was in a stable condition I spoke to the psychiatric team who were called in to assess me. I had no idea what I was saying to them, but many years later I contacted the hospital and asked for a copy of the report. I had said I saw no other way out. That I knew I was hurting my loved ones so much and that I wanted them to be free. Especially my husband. I also told them how concerned I was to still be here, and knew I would be a burden on my family. Some of the people that I worked with at the apple orchard came to see me. I was dreadfully embarrassed.

When I was released from the hospital J and I moved back to Ashburton to be closer to his family and my sister. I was referred to a psychiatric nurse there who I worked with for a couple of months before being referred to a counsellor when I was considered more stable. How do you come back from that? I didn't know.

I remember about three months later thinking to myself that I must have survived for a reason. There must be a plan for my life, a plan I knew nothing about. Perhaps I could use my experiences to help others?

I desperately wanted to see my mother. I managed to talk to her on the phone occasionally, but the lines in Zimbabwe were very unpredictable. None of J's family or mine would talk to me about what had happened. I guess they didn't know what to say, but I felt as though I had shamed them in some way. I worked with a wonderful counsellor from America called Yolanda for a while. I would meet with her once a week. She was the only person I opened up to. The only person I was honest about my feelings with. We worked together for about eight months.

Sometimes, when I had time to myself, I would drive out to the local beach and spend time there alone. No one knew I was there. My husband was working, I used to drop him off and he'd get a lift back, and my parents-in-law were working too. They were lonely times. I would stare out across the ocean and wonder what would become of me. Would I ever forgive myself? Would J ever love me again? I didn't dare let myself think of Zimbabwe. That door had shut forever.

The truth is I didn't forgive myself, and although I knew my husband loved me in a way, there was always a barrier. Was he with me because of duty or because he wanted to be? Was he too afraid to leave in case I repeated what I'd already done once? Those questions whirled around my head.

But, life has a way of just carrying on, and soon enough the time came for me to look for work.

****

CHAPTER TWENTY-ONE
Stepping into the New

"Let go of things you can't change, focus on things you can."
Anon

While I'd been training as a fitness instructor in Motueka I'd met a lady from Ashburton during one of the face to face training weekends that made up the course. We'd stayed in contact and once I felt up to talking to people I rang her to tell her I was now living in Ashburton. She invited me to her property which was about ten minutes away from the town centre. She lived in a beautiful old house with a huge garden. She asked me why we'd moved down, and I burst into tears and told her everything. She gave me the biggest, longest hug, and from that day forth was a loyal friend. Her name was Louisa.

She knew someone that worked in the local health shop and found out that there was some temporary work going there as one of the staff members was going on a cruise. Incredibly nervous, I walked in one day and introduced myself. I said I'd heard about the position and would I be able to apply. My friend's contact helped me and I was given the job.

For the first time since leaving Zimbabwe, I glimpsed a life that I might enjoy. My boss was a wonderfully kind man with a great sense of humour. They welcomed me into their working family and I felt I had some purpose again. I'd always been interested in herbs and supplements and the environment was very positive.

Unfortunately, another blow was waiting round the corner — my sister and her partner were on the move — to the UK. I was devastated, and even though I knew it was their life, I felt deserted. We said our teary farewells and they departed.

My temporary stint at the health shop came to an end when the person I was filling in for came home. Although I was still called in to do the occasional shift, I had no idea what to do next. Fortunately, luck appeared to be on my side as the staff member that had returned put in her notice and I was offered the job again. It was only part time which was perfect for me because I still had a very low threshold for stress and probably wouldn't have coped well with full time work. J was working night shifts at the local meat packers at this stage. He hated it, and I really felt for him. We hardly saw each other, however it paid the bills. Because we were still on work permits we didn't have access to the public health system and all the costs incurred during my time in hospital had gone onto our credit card. Through his hard work we managed to pay it off. Fortunately, he didn't have to stay in that job too long. When one came up in the local mobile phone store he applied and was accepted. The role in time lead to a business opportunity and he became the store owner.

Not long after I started my job Louisa asked me if I wanted to open up a circuit training business with her. There was an old church up for rent and she wanted to use it. I loved the idea and said 'yes' immediately. We called it: 'Fitness to Wellness.'

They were fun days. Growing up in Zimbabwe, I was raised to be self-employed, having a job wasn't really something I'd ever considered, so the opportunity now to do something like this was ideal.

Louisa and I spent hours working in that church together. I remember the old tape deck we had for music. Tunes from the 80s blared out during the sessions and the ladies loved it, as it was an older age group that we worked with. In between classes we would grab a latte at the local cafe.

In the winter months we would light a fire in the church's huge old fireplace. Louisa's husband owned a second hand furniture store and she'd picked out an old lounge suite for us. It was homely, light hearted and most importantly, fun.

I'm not sure what happened; when things started to go wrong. I think it might have been me. In fact, I'm sure it was. I was finding working at the health shop and the circuit centre too much. I was getting really tired and dreaded having to take classes. I didn't know how to tell Louisa; I didn't want to hurt her feelings. So I wrote her a letter and said I was pulling out of the partnership. She wasn't happy about it, but we remained friends and she continued the centre on her own.

I look back on that and I wonder if maybe it was because I was actually happy there that I pulled out. I know it doesn't make sense but I mistrusted happiness, and rather than embrace it, I ran away from it. I was suspicious of anything that appeared too easy.

Not long after that 'escape,' a full time position became available at the health shop and I jumped at it. This time I was running the store, doing the ordering, reports, staff training and courses. It was vibrant, exciting and empowering. I would spend hours studying herbs, vitamins and minerals, and I devoured every course I could lay my hands on. I was very comfortable selling products that would help people get better and I loved working with the customers.

But, I remember that there was still anxiety and fear in my world. I took a lot of supplements for stress. Kava Kava, melatonin, B complex. I'm sure I'd tried everything in the store before too long.

I didn't have a life outside of work. I had my garden, and took care of our home, but I had no social life or friends apart from Louisa.

I wasn't drinking so I couldn't go anywhere near places that smelt of alcohol without having a panic attack. I didn't go out with J because I hated being around anyone that was drinking. I knew he was disappointed in me but I couldn't put myself through that again. So I stayed home. I wrote a lot in those days. I couldn't write about my past but I wrote poetry and musings. Writing was always a comfort.

I also had a beautiful cat to keep me company. She was found as a kitten in the Ashburton Arcade where the health shop I worked in was. No one wanted her so I took her home, and called her 'Chicken' because she was so timid. They say cats don't have owners, but Chicken definitely knew she was mine. She was a tabby cat, and had long hair.

Sadly, I had little contact with my family. My sister had given birth to a baby boy and I desperately wished I could've been there for her.

After a couple of years, I grew bored with the health shop. I'd done as much learning as I could in that environment and I wanted more. I explored herbal medicine and naturopathy but the courses were all too long. I wanted something I could master quickly.

Saying goodbye to the health shop was difficult, but I knew I had to. Once again the guilt kicked in. Did I let them down? I was oddly bereft after leaving; all this time on my hands and nothing to do with it.

My sister offered to pay for me to go over and stay with her in Belfast, Northern Ireland where she was living with her family. I hadn't seen her in five years and it was an opportunity I couldn't turn down. It was only for three weeks so I went alone.

Before I went away I set about reconnecting with friends in the UK; friends that had emigrated there when the troubles in Zimbabwe started. I hadn't been in contact with them for many years. It stirred some deep memories and nostalgia for the life I'd once had back in Zimbabwe.

After a horrendously long flight I arrived at Belfast City airport where my sister, her partner and their son were waiting to meet me. The moment I came into the airport lounge and saw them waiting for me will be etched in my mind forever. I tried not to cry but tears rolled down my cheeks unbidden. I saw my nephew Bradley for the first time; an adorable, happy little boy of three and he gave me the biggest smile. My heart melted.

Three amazing weeks followed. We talked of Zimbabwe; of days gone by. We sat up till the wee hours playing monopoly, laughing and bonding again almost like never before. They were precious moments. I told Vicky I was unhappy in my marriage, that I didn't trust J, didn't feel loved by him. The words I used were: 'you know when a child gets tired of a toy? It bores them, but they still don't want to part with it? That's how I think he sees me.' It was so wonderful to be around people who were interested in who I was, who listened to what I had to say. Around them I felt I mattered, and I realised how I never felt like that around my husband. My sister asked me to stay. I truly wished I could but I knew I couldn't do that to J. I knew I needed to do something though. The trip had truly brought home to me how suppressed I was. I thought of all the times I'd tried to talk to J about things that interested me, only to be met by deaf ears, or a smart, condescending remark. An introvert by nature it only took a certain number of snide comments before I gave up and that's what I'd done —given up.

Reluctantly, I boarded the plane back to New Zealand and J met me at the airport. He must have known straight away something had changed. I didn't want to talk to him about it immediately, but I had to. I wanted a trial separation. He pleaded with me to stay, told me how much he'd missed me and how much he loved me — so I agreed to stay. I didn't want to. I knew I wasn't honouring my feelings but I didn't know what else to do, the alternative was too hard to bear. All I wanted was for us both to be happy.

I talked to him about how I had felt in the marriage and for a while things were better. He seemed to understand and to genuinely want to work on our relationship. But it wasn't long before we were back where we'd been before, and I buried myself in my studies, and after looking into many different courses, I decided it was time to have horses in my life again so I chose to train as an Equine Bowen therapist. My life was off on yet another tangent.

****

CHAPTER TWENTY-TWO
Studies and a new path

"The horse is a mirror to your soul. Sometimes you might not like what you see. Sometimes you will."
Buck Brannaman

In order to work with horses, it was compulsory to first train as a Bowen therapist for humans. I wasn't keen on this at all, however it had to be done. The first part of the training took four days and in those four days I went from never wanting to work on people to wanting to build a practice for people alongside the equine business. The couple that trained me were so self aware and grounded that it rubbed off on me. They supported me in every way and I remember thinking, 'this is amazing, I will always have their support as I move forward as a therapist.' And I did. Even today they remain in contact with me.

About two months after the human Bowen started I flew to Hamilton, on the North Island of New Zealand to do the first stage of the equine training. Once again I found myself part of a supportive group of therapists and it was wonderful. One of the women on the course was from the South Island like me and we developed a friendship that continues today.

Being in contact with horses again was a boost for my soul. I'd forgotten how much I loved them. There's something healing about horses, they have a simple, straightforward way of being, of accepting you and inviting you to grow. As the quote at the beginning of the chapter reads they mirror your soul. I remember the first few times I worked on a horse during the course, my heart opened again after years of being shut away and I couldn't stem the tears of gratitude.

Around the same time as I was training I'd started to ride again, and I'd leased a young mare who was half Friesian, half thoroughbred, called Twiggy. She was a beautiful horse and I learnt so much from her. She challenged me to be strong because she had a very dominant personality. Unfortunately, she was probably not the best choice for a nervous rider just starting back so I didn't keep her long.

Over the course of the next year I completed my human Bowen training and the equine training alongside it. I was required to do twenty equine case studies and I remember with affection the four-legged families I became part of during that year, and the owners who welcomed me into their worlds.

My first one was a beautiful, noble, black gelding. He was a dressage horse and lived on a property about ten minutes away from my home. I ended up treating most of the horses at that farm over time, and also doing some work on the owner's husband who competed in triathlons. He was a remarkably fit and healthy man, but tragically he developed pancreatic cancer two years later and passed away after a long fight. When I went to his funeral I sat at the back of the church with tears of remembrance in my eyes; I knew what it was like to lose someone you love after a harrowing battle.

A favourite place to go for my case studies was a property about twenty minutes away that was owned by a man who did rodeo commentating and trained horses in natural horsemanship. The reason I loved this property was because I was able to go into the paddock alone to work on the horses. Left to my own devices I could really tune in to the animal I was working on. I remember one of the horses was a dear little skewbald mare who was in foal for the first time. She had a peaceful energy, and I felt as though she was telling me how proud she was that she was going to be a mum.

I cried a lot when I worked on horses. There was a lot of sadness still locked in my body that needed to be healed and horses provided the perfect therapy. I was able to get back in touch with myself, something I hadn't done in years. However, I was afraid and would only go so far. I was afraid that if I went too deep I would reach a place where I had to take action, and I wasn't ready for that. So I allowed my heart to be nurtured by the warmth of equine allowance and felt honoured to be able to help them in return.

I loved completing my human case studies too. I had to do a hundred, but it didn't have to be a hundred different people, just treatments. One of my case studies was a man who had degenerative disc disease. I would treat him every week and in return he taught me how to play the guitar. I had always wanted to learn guitar; it was a great trade.

I remember feeling that helping people to heal was my purpose in life. I wanted to be the best practitioner I could be. I felt sad in a way though as I learnt all these new skills and helped strangers, because I also wanted to help my mother, but couldn't.

The year went very fast and it wasn't long before I was a qualified equine and human Bowen therapist. I felt very proud of myself, it'd been a challenging year and I had come out the other end ready to step into my own practise.

Just down the road from me was an acupuncture clinic and I rented a room there. The owner was a very kind lady, and a brilliant acupuncturist. She was Chinese and had trained with one of the top trainers in China. I had great plans. Business was slow at the start, but it soon built up. I would go to all the local horse shows and put flyers on people's windscreens. I sponsored a couple of competitions and did demonstrations at a pony club and I remember my excitement when I got my first booking. I made up all my own marketing material, did talks at various events and would walk around the town putting flyers into people's letter boxes; it took hours but did lead to new clients.

****

CHAPTER TWENTY-THREE
Reconnecting

"A summer I will always remember with people I will never forget."
Anon

Just after I qualified and set up my practise I flew to Belfast again to see my sister. My husband had wanted to come with me but his visa didn't arrive in time so once again I flew alone. This trip marked a very special occasion as I was going to see my mother again after nine years' separation. She had already travelled to Belfast before me.

On arrival at the airport I walked through the passenger terminal to greet my sister and her family who were waiting for me; my mother was nowhere to be seen. I asked Vicky where she was and she told me that mother had been too nervous to greet me. Vicky went off to call her and the next thing I knew my mother was walking towards me. We hold images in our minds of how people were when we last saw them so it came as quite a shock to see her again.

My pictures were of the mother I'd known as a child; the mother I was never good enough for. But, here, in front of me was a woman much older than I remembered, thinner than I remembered and showing clear signs of having had a hard and emotionally challenging life. We cried in each other's arms and I experienced some really painful emotions. I could see clearly that in the time I'd been away she'd been to hell and back. She'd never spoken to me or written about her experiences in Zimbabwe, and I think because it was so hard being miles away from her I'd blocked it out and tried not to think about it.

Now of course, with her right in front of me, it hit me like a ton of bricks, and I was appalled at myself for having abandoned her. I wanted to wash away the distress that was etched on her face. I was furious she'd been subjected to so much agony. She was purely an innocent woman who wanted nothing more than to live in peace on the farm she loved.

She didn't tell us much about what she'd been through, and what she did tell us needed to remain between us, so I won't repeat any of it here. However, I noticed that she was very nervous and apologised all the time; not the mother I remembered at all.

She did say that the farm was in a bad way. There was no hot water or even running water upstairs. She had to carry buckets up each night. I wanted to spoil her as much as possible so it was wonderful to be able to take her out for meals, buy her clothes and care for her.

We talked a lot during that time and inevitably my childhood came up. She spoke of the emotional turmoil she'd faced when she'd first handed me over to a full time nanny and how she never felt we'd bonded. She knew that I thought she didn't love me as much as Vicky, but she assured me that wasn't the case at all. I can remember her saying this to me quite clearly, but interestingly, it's hard to accept that things were different once those beliefs have been embedded, and I frankly didn't believe her.

Although I felt for her after what she'd been through I was still angry that she'd not been there for me after I'd tried to end my life.

If I ever have children, I told myself, things will be different.

My sister and I took her to see her old childhood friend, my godmother, and to visit places she'd not seen for many years. I wanted her to stay in Belfast, in fact I begged her to stay. But her commitment to Melfort was too strong.

The time we spent together passed too quickly and soon the day came for teary farewells. Mother and I were travelling to London together, then she was taking a connecting flight back to Harare while I travelled to Cheltenham for a few days to stay with the lady who'd developed the equine Bowen course.

We sat next to each other on the plane and she told me again how much she loved me and how sorry she was for being such a distant mother. That flight was hard. I would have preferred her to stay in the UK; her going back to the wilds of Africa alone broke my heart. I tried to understand why she couldn't stay, but I couldn't. To me the decision seemed simple, family comes first. For her it was more complicated. Something had happened during her time alone there, something I would never understand but would simply have to accept. She felt obligated to the farm, to the country, and to the people.

We reached London and were faced with the enormity of our possibly final farewell. I couldn't cry. I had to be strong or I knew I would never make it to Cheltenham. I was very aware that I might never see my mother again.

I bit my tongue and held her tightly as we said our goodbyes. When my granny was alive she had always said in moments such as this 'anything unsaid, said' which was simply a way of avoiding having to say too much in an emotional situation. We said that, and went our separate ways.

In a daze I arrived in Cheltenham and was met at the station by the lovely lady that developed the European School of Equine Bowen. She took me to her beautiful home and over the next few days showed me around the Cotswolds. I wasn't really present though, my mind was far away. But soon enough, I was on the plane heading back to New Zealand once again.

****

CHAPTER TWENTY-FOUR
The plains of emptiness

"I wanted to write down exactly how I felt, but somehow the page stayed empty, and I could not have described it any better."
WTM

The next two years were spent working my business and building my client base. I've struggled to write about those years and upon self inquiry I realise it was because they were years when I felt flat and empty. I tried to find joy in my work. I worked long hours, often leaving home at 6.30 in the morning to return exhausted at 8 or 9 pm.

I wasn't feeling loved and supported at home, and I looked to my business to bring me what I yearned for. Of course, it didn't, all that happened was that I began to slowly but surely burn out.

About half way through this period I received a phone call from a racehorse owner in Australia who wanted me to treat his New Zealand team. I didn't know then but he was one of Australia's most prominent owners, and his horses were trained by Mark Purdon, one of New Zealand's top trainers. I felt so nervous the first time I drove into their very smart yard to meet him! He showed me around and took me to the horses that I was to work on. I needn't have worried because from that day on I was left to my own devices whenever I was called in to treat an animal.

The owner had a large team that was constantly growing and it wasn't long before the team became my main source of business in the equine field. I worked on the horses weekly most of the time and developed quite a rapport with them, particularly Arden Rooney and Crackers. These two were gentle and they absolutely loved their treatments. As I was always alone when I worked on them I would often talk to them about my life.

Alongside the equine business was my 'people' clinic which ticked along nicely. Because I lived in a small town it never really grew to more than a day a week but I didn't mind. What was interesting about the work was that it seemed to be turning into more of a life-coaching business. People always seemed to be able to talk to me about their problems and challenges, and most sessions were a combination of thirty minutes of coaching followed by a Bowen treatment.

I also did a lot of work with infants and young children. They responded so well to Bowen, and were amazing to work with. Because adults can have so much baggage they often require several treatments and lifestyle changes before results are seen, whereas children respond immediately.

One of my young clients was the daughter of a lady who lived on a farm very close to my home. They were a very horsey family and soon I was treating the whole family plus the horses. I became friends with the girl's mother whose name was Annabelle.

I loved going to their property, it reminded me so much of Melfort. There were chickens running around, horses everywhere, and the atmosphere was relaxed. Time stood still there.

Annabelle offered me the opportunity to ride again and I accepted. I learnt so much working with her. She was very much into natural horsemanship and I went on my first clinic there. It was over two days and was taken by Ken Dromgool. Ken was from Paihia in the Bay of Islands, way up the top of the North Island. He'd worked with horses all his life, training with the famous Ray Hunt in America. Ken's knowledge was incredible and I learnt a great deal from him.

Not long after the clinic Buck Brannaman visited New Zealand and held a clinic in Christchurch. I went with Annabelle and her daughter as an observer. It was the year that the movie about him called *Buck* had been released and seeing him live was amazing. He had the ability to truly communicate with horses in a way that not many people can. I was forever inspired by him.

I helped Annabelle with her young horses that were just coming in to work, as I had done at Melfort with ours as a child. I felt very privileged to work with horses in this way again, and I thought it would have brought me more joy and happiness, yet I still felt empty. I look back now and see it was because I felt desperately lonely at home. My marriage lacked emotional closeness and I think I tried to substitute it with time spent among the horses at Annabelle's farm.

My husband and I lead virtually separate lives, having very different interests. Often I tried to talk to him about it. I asked if we could do more together, go out more together and try to rekindle connection. But, he wasn't interested and I took it very personally, blamed myself for everything and thought that maybe if I changed who I was he would be happier.

It's a very draining and painful place to be, the place where you feel you're not enough. There was just this endless flatness, and it was killing me slowly but surely. We all need intimacy and closeness in life, it's part of our nature. To be shut out by someone you love is incredibly difficult to bear. Now of course, I realise he must've been going through his own issues, but I didn't see that then.

I also didn't trust him. Intuition told me there was something wrong, yet I could never pinpoint what it was. I felt so guilty not trusting him, all I wanted was open and clear communication between us but there was just this invisible wall.

****

CHAPTER TWENTY-FIVE
Pregnancy

"Mummy are you ready, my life is just about to start. I will hold your little finger, but you will hold my heart."
Anon

J had wanted children for some time, it was me who'd put it off. One night I was sitting in the bath and I found myself thinking about my age, and I knew the time had come. Despite warnings from well-meaning people that it might take some time for me to conceive, it happened very fast.

Lucy was conceived in 2011 and at Christmas all the family were told. I remember the first time I heard her heart beat through the scanner. I wept with joy. Falling pregnant and realising I was going to bring a new life into the world was almost overwhelming. Yet there was a part of me that was scared stiff. Never having had any maternal instincts prior to this I was apprehensive - what if I was a bad mother? What if I didn't know what to do and my child grew up feeling like I had? I made a promise to myself in that first trimester that my child would be raised very differently.

I read a beautiful book called, *'The Continuum Concept'* written in 1975 by Jean Liedloff. She'd spent two and a half years in the South American jungle studying a stone age Indian tribe called the Yequana. Her study was based on their parenting system. Having watched the tribe for some time she became aware of how different the children were to children in western society. They were calmer, happier and more grounded. They showed none of the emotional reactions and issues western children displayed such as anxiety, throwing tantrums, shyness and so on. She was very impressed by their mental, physical and emotional vitality. The key difference between the Yequana children and western children lay in the fact that they never experienced separation. They were always included in community life and kept in close physical contact with their parents or carer. The book touched me profoundly as it reminded me of what my childhood hadn't been. I knew these principles would be the foundation of my parenting.

About six weeks before my due date one of my scans came back slightly abnormal. The placental blood flow wasn't a hundred percent and further tests were required. I flipped straight into panic. I'd wanted a water birth, and had planned to take homeopathics for pain relief instead of allopathic medicine. The abnormal scan totally jeopardised my plan. I became quite stressed. At about the same time J had a rugby accident and broke two of his fingers. I had to take him in my heavily pregnant state up to Christchurch hospital for surgery. It was quite major surgery at that. Following it, he had to see a hand specialist regularly to help with regaining normal function of his fingers. Between the two of us it felt like we were forever at the hospital!

Further tests and scans showed that I had amnio hyramnios, which means too much amniotic fluid. That explained why I was so enormous! The combination of that and the placental issues lead the doctors to recommend an induction. The date was set for two weeks' time.

I was so nervous! I scared myself silly doing something I recommend no woman ever should do, and that was researching the complications and process involved in induced labour.

On 11th July, 2012, I was admitted to Christchurch Women's Hospital and labour was induced. The next day, after an excruciating battle my beautiful little baby girl was born. I will never forget the moment she was placed in my arms. A perfect little bundle; just over 6 pounds. I cried, J cried, it was a moment that will be etched on both our memories forever. Her tiny fingers wrapped around mine and I understood. I understood what it meant to have your heart walking outside your body. Because of the complications in the last stages of labour I stayed in the hospital for three days.

Everyday, J would spend as much time with us as possible. Together, we cherished the first moments with our child. Both of us were absolutely besotted. I remember the first bath, and how afraid we were that we would hurt her. How clumsy we were! Her tiny little hands would have fitted into my palm at least three times.

Nothing had prepared me for the love I felt for my baby.

After three days I was transferred to Ashburton hospital for a further three. I was fortunate to have so much time in hospital as I was shattered after the traumatic labour. Babies were something I knew absolutely nothing about and having the nurses there to show me what to do was a blessing. So many people came to see us; bringing us gifts and flowers. It was a very emotional time for both of us.

****

CHAPTER TWENTY-SIX
Motherhood

"Walk alongside me mama, and hold my little hand. I have so many things to learn, that I don't yet understand."
Anon

After a week in hospital I was finally discharged and J collected us. Driving home that day with our beautiful little bundle is a memory I will treasure forever. J had prepared the house for us; immaculate and toasty warm. It needed to be, it was the middle of winter.

My neighbour came round to welcome us home. I haven't written much about her yet. Her name was Ellen. Although she'd lived next door all along it was only when I was pregnant that we began to develop a friendship, and she'd helped me no end before Lucy was born. We both shared a love of gardening and I'll never forget how she spent an entire weekend helping me put pea straw on all my beds to prepare them for the winter.

She knitted the most exquisite clothes for wee Lucy and her support and kindness is something I'll never forget. It's not often in life someone goes out of their way for you with no expectations of anything in return. Ellen is such a person.

As Lucy grew. Ellen became like a grandmother to her and Lucy adored her. She was also, and still is a very close friend.

Her support when I found out about my husband's affair was something I'm eternally grateful for. I frequently went over to her house in floods of tears and she always listened, always cared and helped me with Lucy.

The first few weeks at home were a complete blur because I caught a nasty tummy bug and was quite ill. As a result, Lucy had to go on a bottle, and with this her issues with colic started.

I became increasingly frustrated with doctors and midwives telling me that what she was going through was quite normal and to continue with the feeding routine I was following. I took her to a cranial osteopath and had several treatments done. I also did a lot of Bowen therapy on her myself but she was still very unsettled.

I remember the many occasions I would be helpless and in tears in the lounge holding my screaming baby and not knowing what was wrong. I refused to believe this was normal so I did my own research. Based on that information I started her on a goats' milk formula and the change was instant. Bingo, lactose intolerance. This was later confirmed when I had a hair analysis done.

I'd heard there are babies that sleep through the night right from the start. Lucy, obviously, wasn't one of them, and nothing prepared me for the effects of sleep deprivation. I didn't agree with the suggested cry-it-out methods so I didn't have a full night's sleep for nearly two years.

But the funny thing was I coped. I guess because I had to. Plus, there were so many moments with Lucy that took my breath away and made it all worthwhile. Like the first time she held my gaze. The first time she smiled, and uttered her first word.

It's amazing how someone so small can touch a heart so deeply. J and I shared so many precious moments with her. The laughter at meal times, the giggles. The first crawls and wobbly stands. The bath time games when she would crawl hell-for-leather down the passage in an attempt to escape, squeaking with delight only to find one of us waiting for her which resulted in a quick about turn and repeat procedure in the opposite direction.

I remember once looking out of the window and seeing the rows of tiny little clothes on the washing line. I felt so very content. I thought that at last I would have what I'd always yearned for.

When I became a mother something changed in me. It triggered a deep awareness of myself as a little girl and although it has taken me years to understand what that meant, I know it began the moment she was born. I would look at her lying in her pram, completely helpless, totally dependent on me for absolutely everything, and I remembered my own childhood and how emotionally neglected I'd felt. I made the decision then that Lucy would never experience the same.

When she was four months old, I started doing a bit of work again. It's funny, before she was born I'd said that I would return to full time work when she was three months old and put her into full time care. That was before she truly captured my heart! I could hardly bear to leave her for the few hours twice a week! But it was nice to get some time to myself and also realise that I could balance motherhood with a business.

In April 2013, my mother came to visit again and met her granddaughter for the first time. She was with us just three short weeks. It was interesting watching her around Lucy and seeing that though she obviously loved her she was not overly confident or comfortable around such a small child. I gleaned a better understanding of how she must've felt when I was small. Lucy crawled for the first time while mother was with us. Perfect timing!

It was also while my mother was staying that I started to become aware of the fact that J was not as present around the family as he had been. I thought perhaps it was because mother was there, but it continued after she left. I started to worry. My work was getting busier and I was beginning to burn out with the sleepless nights. He said everything was fine but I knew it wasn't. Resentment welled up as I cared for Lucy almost alone; everything was being left to me.

I had signed up to do an equine massage course on the North Island in July. Lucy came with me, accompanied by Yvonne who'd kindly agreed to care for Lucy while I attended the training. Yvonne was J's sister's mother-in-law. We flew to Palmerston North and stayed with friends who lived on a dairy farm there. I completed five intensive days of learning while Lucy stayed in Voni's capable hands. We returned to

Ashburton and when I got home I knew there had been a shift in my marriage. I just couldn't pinpoint what it was.

The next five months were tense to say the least. I was fighting my own suspicions that J was up to something. At the same time, I was attempting to complete the case studies for my course, care for Lucy and run my business. My stress levels were pretty high. By the time December came around and I found out what was going on I had lost all motivation to finish the course.

****

CHAPTER TWENTY-SEVEN
And then there was chaos

"Life constantly presents the greatest opportunity brilliantly disguised as the biggest disaster."
David Icke

I read the above quote and smile, for when the chaos hit I didn't see any great changes on the horizon. All I saw was an endless valley of despair. But in the thick of chaos one cannot see very far at all.

Discovering my husband's affair was something words can't describe. If it hadn't been for my daughter I'm not sure I would've survived. But I did, and now, as I look back I can see that though it may sound strange the pain was one of the greatest gifts I've ever been given. If I'd not gone through it, if my heart hadn't been ripped out, I would never have embarked on this incredible journey to my soul. For that I am grateful.

You see, we don't like change. Even though I was unhappy, and I knew I was unhappy, I was too scared to step through it and make a different choice; especially after having my daughter. It is so much easier to stick with the known, even if the known is empty and lifeless. I thought having her would change things and although there was the illusion of change for a period it didn't. I felt committed to making things work for her, to force myself to be happy. But inside I still felt unsupported and knew something was wrong. It's amazing how we can lie to ourselves so much that we actually start to believe it. I kept telling myself it was all in my mind, that it was my fault. I didn't believe I could cope alone, and so even when the truth was right in front of me I pretended not to see it.

But there's something I've come to realise. We are so very much stronger than we know, and we are never given a challenge that we can't overcome. When the chaos appears to be at its most uncontrollable; that is when the greatest growth can occur. No matter what is happening to us on the outside, there is always an inner light that is trying to guide us home. All that we need to do is turn our attention inwards and ask.

There is only one constant in life, and that is change. The key is learning to live life in the space of a question. Learning to be OK with not knowing; and truly understanding that all things will pass.

They always pass. It's hard to see it at the time, but the only way is through the storm.

There is a place deep within us where the love and peace is endless; where we're safe, no matter what's going on outside of us.

It's a place I now call home.

****

PART THREE

COMING HOME

"To be yourself in a world that is constantly trying to make you something else is the greatest accomplishment."

Ralph Waldo Emerson

CHAPTER TWENTY-EIGHT
Core Beliefs

"Whether by action or spoken word, parents are the implements that write the story of a child's future."
Randi J Fine

As I wrote about my life in the surrendering step I became more and more aware of common themes that kept showing up.

- Depression
- Lack of self worth
- Not being enough or worthy of love.
- Not feeling safe to express myself.
- Responsible for other people's feelings

These were the main ones. It all started to click. I saw how the belief systems I'd formed in the first five years of my life had become the filters through which every experience I would have for the rest of my life would go through.

Wow, I thought to myself, just wow.

They were the lens through which I perceived my life. This concept fascinated me. I spent hours and hours researching it, devouring every article I could find on core beliefs. Out of all the research that was done, this was the common finding: Children blame everything on themselves, they don't understand that it's not their fault when their parents are angry or upset and consequently their needs are not met. And this includes the parents' financial difficulties, neglect, abuse, even illness in the family. Children cement this into their psyche in the first five to seven years of life.

Because every family has problems all children will develop some negative core beliefs about themselves, and they become a huge part of the child's personality, and are self perpetuating. Once set deep in the subconscious the brain will continue to search for evidence that supports its beliefs.

In surrendering I was able to see the fundamental beliefs that I'd set and how they'd impacted my life. My belief that I wasn't enough, wasn't lovable and wasn't wanted by my mother affected every relationship I'd ever had. If someone said, 'you're so wonderful, I love you so much,' I would twist it and think, 'if they knew who I really was they wouldn't love me.' I was unable to have deep, open and meaningful relationships because of this. I always put myself down and played small.

I didn't even realise I was doing it until now. That's the scary thing, it's so ingrained we don't even know it's happening.

Another thing that children do when they start to believe something is 'wrong' with them is they begin to suppress their true self and they develop a different self, a 'coping' self. The true self is one's true feelings, personality, dreams, loves, hates and so on. The coping self is the one that tries to mould itself to its environment in order to get its needs met. I used to say what I thought my parents wanted me to say. I would look to my environment to show me how to think, feel and behave. I started to do this when I was about four years old — at least that's what I remember. I became very skilled at it, but it was an incredibly exhausting and painful way to live. It led to something very sad, and that was me forgetting who I was. I forgot my true nature, my true feelings, my dreams and the music of my soul. On a subconscious level I know that I knew something wasn't right, but the patterns were so ingrained that I didn't understand what was really underneath it all. Until now.

From a very young age my thinking patterns went something like this: 'Mummy is not happy, it must be my fault. Something must be wrong with me, I need to be someone else.'

Beliefs such as this alter the course of a lifetime. I know, because it altered mine. In no way do I blame my parents or feel I've been a victim, it was just the way it was. I spent my life up until now trying to be someone I wasn't. Trying to be what I thought people wanted me to be. It's no wonder I turned to drugs, became depressed, suffered from anxiety and starved myself! How could I have possibly known what other people wanted me to be? I didn't, and that was the issue. It was all in my perception. I tried to read people's thoughts, body language and words, then act accordingly. I completely lost touch with myself. Lost the ability to act spontaneously, have fun, let go and just be. I never felt truly happy. I lived in constant fear and worry. Afraid of upsetting people, afraid to say no, worrying about what people thought, worrying about not being enough. It was absolutely exhausting yet I thought it was me! I burnt myself out in my business trying to please everyone. I felt guilty taking time out so I didn't.

All that changed when I made that self inquiry and then surrendered. There was something so incredibly beautiful about moving through the illusion and reconnecting with my true self. I literally felt my heart start to open, like a rose bud slowly unfolding and reaching up to the light.

I cried a lot as I started to reconnect. Tears would flow down my cheeks for the little girl that I had been. I remember many occasions when I would bawl my eyes out and just say, 'I'm so sorry.' It took a lot of courage to make this inner journey, to face my demons, to let myself revisit the places I'd hidden away deep inside and allow the healing I'd never undertaken before to take place.

Yet the beauty and light that came out of it all was absolutely breath-taking. I saw my childhood with completely new eyes. Instead of seeing it as a painful and traumatic time I could see the joy and laughter that'd been there too. Yes, there were some really hard times, but there was also so much more.

I still have moments when I say what I think people want me to say, rather than what I truly feel, but I'm OK with that, because I recognise what I'm doing and don't judge it as wrong. It took 36 years to get where I am now, I'm not going to shake those deep habits in an instant. It's a moment to moment thing. Awareness of it means you are half way there; it just takes practice.

I can see my mother with new eyes too. Instead of seeing her through the eyes of a suppressed child I can now see her through the eyes of awareness and love. You know I spent so long thinking I was responsible for her happiness. Now I see clearly that we are responsible only for our own. Other people's issues are actually none of our business. I remember in one of Marianne Williamson's talks she said, 'stay on your side of the net.' I didn't get it straight away, but I do now. Tend to your own garden and let others tend to theirs.

The same applied to J. One night I had a dream. In the dream he was sitting in one of the bedrooms at Melfort with suitcases round him. He was leaving. I walked into the room and sat down a short distance from him. I said to him, 'I'm glad you married me. I'm grateful for all I learnt from our relationship. Most of all I feel so blessed we created such a beautiful little girl, thank you, and I forgive you.' I woke up and my eyes were full of tears. I walked downstairs still crying and wrote this. Suddenly, it all became so clear to me. Why he'd done what he did. Why he'd hurt me and why we'd remained together so long. Clearly I saw the early days — my drinking, my pain and my woundedness. He was there, always there. I'll never forget how he stayed when most people would've run a mile. I know now that some of the things that happened between us are things I would never allow in my life again, but back then I was only treated the way I believed

I deserved to be treated. That doesn't make it OK, but it does mean that I can now see it for what it truly was, and forgive. I can also see how it may have looked from his perspective, and have gratitude and awe for how much he put up with, and still stayed at my side.

Forgiveness is something we do for ourselves. I think I was afraid to begin; that if I forgave it meant that I was condoning what'd happened, saying that how I'd been treated was OK. However, I've can see that this isn't the case at all. Forgiveness frees you from the burden of the past. It frees you from your hurts and wounds and allows you to be present. It is impossible to be fully in each moment whilst carrying resentment, anger and pain.

Another thing forgiveness does is it allows you to take back your power. It took me a long time to really understand this, but in terms of growth it's vital. Holding on to what someone did to you actually gives that person power over you. You believe that you're not able to be truly happy because they wounded you. In other words, your happiness is hindered because of them. This is not true. Happiness comes from within and actually has nothing to do with anything anyone else does at all.

One of the most powerful areas in which we can help this planet move from fear to love is through the children. They enter this world as vessels of pure love and while they are with us, their parents, it's our responsibility to keep them that way.

My parents did the best they could, they raised me the way their parents raised them, and I hold absolutely nothing against them for that. I believe that when we are adults we can choose for ourselves and blaming our parents is just an excuse for not to take responsibility for our own lives.

But when the core beliefs of childhood are so deeply embedded in our subconscious that we don't even realise they're there, it becomes more difficult, in fact, impossible.

If as adults we could become more aware of the vulnerability of children, particularly in the first five years of life, and then act on that awareness and change parenting approaches, how would future generations change? Imagine children who were raised to believe they were invincible? Beautiful, creative, amazing beings of love? How much unnecessary pain would they avoid if this was the case? What amazing gifts would they share with the world? What a different place this world would be.

We would never speak to another adult in the way some of us speak to little children. What makes us think they are less deserving of our respect and understanding? They are even more so as they have no way of escaping or defending themselves as adults can. Western society in general shuts children down, moulds their psyche to fit into what is termed 'acceptable.' It is cruel and it is forced. Children learn it's not OK to express certain emotions, to have certain opinions. They are trained to act in a proscribed way, thus they learn to shut down their true self.

Why? I believe it all comes down to fear. We believe we have to dominate children. Show them we mean business and that we are the boss. We're afraid if we don't we will lose control. So we mould them into what we want, then watch in wonder when they have anger issues, or marry someone that abuses them. Without understanding what we do, we create belief systems that literally map the course of our children's lives.

My daughter has been gifted to me to help me grow on many levels, of that I am convinced. She has a strong temper and is the most determined little girl I know. I watch her, I sit with her through her tantrums, stand back and let her express the myriad emotions that flow out of her. And I can see myself as a little girl so clearly. As she shouts and stamps I hear my father saying, 'children should be seen and not heard.' I hear my mother shouting at me to, 'Shut up! Get out, you horrible child!' I see myself being beaten. I wonder what I would've been like if I'd been allowed to express everything I felt. Would I have been shy? Would I have feared strong emotions as I have for so much of my life? Would I have allowed the abuse in the relationship I endured for too many years? I doubt it.

The frightening thing is, it's so engrained in my psyche that at times it takes huge willpower not to do exactly what they did. That concerns me but I know I would never act on it. I know I've done enough inner work now and have enough awareness not to. But I see how easy it would be to do it, it's built in, like a reflex we have no control over.

One of my deepest wishes would be for adults to look deep within themselves and ask to remember their own less pleasant experiences as children, then choose differently, for their children, for their grandchildren, and for the human race.

****

CHAPTER TWENTY-NINE
The Doors of Perception

"Thought is not reality; yet it is through thought that our realities are created." Sydney Banks

As I write this chapter now, having written and gone through everything in the previous chapters, I see clearly that I had completely given my power away. To my mother, to J, my circumstances, my past. I guess I had always been in victim mode. I believed life happened to me. Now, as I come out the other side I see that actually my life happens 'because of me'. I am the creator of my reality, and I create my reality through my thinking. We all do, we have just forgotten this and have been taught otherwise.

'Everything you have ever wanted is within you.'

This insight came to me one day when I was sitting in nature meditating. It was only when I became truly honest with myself that I realised something incredible; that I had chosen to hold onto thought patterns that no longer served me and created a painful perception of my life. Yes, I had developed core beliefs in childhood. Yes, I had been subjected to painful experiences. However, I chose to hold onto those experiences through my thinking long after the experiences themselves had passed.

I know this may sound confusing, but actually it's very simple. You see, we are raised to believe that our experience of life is created by our external environment when actually it's created by our own thoughts.

How do I know this? I know this because I came to realise that all the painful experiences that had happened to me in the past didn't exist anymore yet they were still very much alive within me, and the only thing that kept them alive was my thoughts. I wasn't even aware that I was thinking them, it was such an unconscious habit. Yet once I became aware of it I was free to choose differently thereby seeing that the past could not hurt me. It had actually never been able to hurt me.

What really helped me to truly understand this principle was the works of philosopher and author Sydney Banks. His book, *'The Missing Link'* had a profound effect on my understanding of thought and how it creates our reality. I thought my experiences were creating the pain and I starved myself and became an alcoholic in an attempt to escape them. Now I see that what I was really trying to escape were my own habitual thinking patterns. It's incredibly liberating to see it this way. To see that we all live in separate realities created by our thoughts; but that our thoughts are not a true representation of reality. They are just our perception in that moment.

I remember for months after my marriage ended crying every time my daughter played a song on her iPad that I'd heard just after finding out about J's affair in New Zealand. I thought this was still emotional trauma coming up for me. But after I became more aware of thought I realised that actually it wasn't the song that was causing the tears — it was the thoughts I'd had when I heard the song. Once I let myself really 'get this' I was able to change the thoughts and consequently my feelings.

I remember one day when I was on the last chapter of the part 'Surrender' a song came on the radio. It was a song by Simply Red called, 'If you don't know me by now.' Simply Red was a band J and I had loved to listen to together in Zimbabwe. I listened to the song from beginning to end, and I didn't cry. I simply smiled, grateful for the memories it had triggered. It was in that moment that I knew I'd got it. I'd made it through what I thought was a battlefield and come out the other side stronger, more powerful and filled with love. I also now saw that in fact, there was no battlefield and there never had been.

If we hadn't stayed together as long as we did our beautiful daughter wouldn't have been born. She was meant to be born, and we were meant to be her parents.

This journey has been the most powerful, life changing journey of my life. I have literally stepped through the doors of perception and instead of finding the monsters I feared were lurking in the shadows waiting to rip me apart, I found the light of my soul and the pieces of my heart I'd forgotten existed.

A song comes to mind, a song my father used to play: *"We had joy, we had fun, we had seasons in the sun. But the wine and the song like the seasons have all gone."*

Sometimes we have to die inside in order to make room for something new. As Einstein said, 'You cannot solve a problem from the same consciousness that created it. You must learn to see the world anew.'

I would perhaps change this slightly and say, 'You must learn to THINK anew.'

Sometimes I used to think I just got stuck in a time warp. Stuck in the first wave of grief and it just snow-balled from there. Never allowing the healing process to even begin, I was tossed on the waves of my own nightmare, one which I tried to escape, but failed.

This understanding enabled me to literally change how I saw my past and my present. I still have negative thoughts, I am human, so I always will. However, now that I see that they're just thoughts, I feel free to not get so caught up in them. It's quite incredible how one's reality can change just through this simple understanding. I remember getting up one morning to the sound of rain. It'd been raining for close on three weeks. I felt down and slightly claustrophobic. Then I looked a little closer at my thoughts and saw that they were negative. I chose to change them and although it obviously still continued to rain I felt better. Not so long ago those feelings could have easily spiralled into something quite dramatic such as me thinking I had to leave the country and seek a new home where it hardly ever rained.

I sigh and take a deep breath. Did I spend years in misery just because of my own thinking? In a way yes I did. Yet I probably wouldn't have understood this back then. Awareness, growth, cannot be forced. It happens when it is meant to happen, and when it is chosen. As the saying goes; 'when the student is ready the teacher will arrive.'

****

CHAPTER THIRTY
Purpose and love

"Built into you is an internal guidance system that shows you the way home. All you need to do is heed the voice."
Neale Donald Walsh

I was sitting at the edge of the lake on a sunny autumn day. I'd been coming to the lake regularly to meditate, and escape the busyness of life. My soul craved it, and the moment I sat down I felt peace embrace me.

A breeze picked up around me, lasting only a few seconds. At the same time, I heard a voice in my head. It was subtle yet clear as a bell. This is what it said: 'I am in everything. I am on the breeze, I am in the grass, I am in tears and I am in laughter, I infuse everything and everything infuses me. I am in you, and you are in me.'

The words took me by surprise. I asked, 'Who are you?'

The answer: 'I am love. I am the beginning, I am the end, I am wisdom, I am insight, I am truth. I have many names, what you call me does not matter. Just know that I am.'

I pondered this for a while. In that beautiful moment I felt connected to Everything. I realised that we are not our thoughts, we are not our feelings, we are not our situations; we are so much more. We are spirit. We are energy. We are everything and we are nothing. In that moment I connected to the universal energy of life.

As I continued to sit in the beautiful stillness of the moment I asked, 'What am I here to do?' The reply: 'coach and write.' The answer slowly sank in and I felt at peace. I felt like I had accessed a very deep place within myself.

Later, I thought, if only we could see how powerful we are — how bright our inner light is. Yet we cling to the darkness, for that is what we're trained to do. We live in fear and don't realise that the only thing that can change us, is us. The more we can awaken to the truth of who we really are, the more we can let our light shine. The light is always there, just behind the darkness; the silver behind the thundercloud.

Some people focus on what they can do to change the world. The biggest gift you can give the world is to be yourself. Be you and change the world! The most profound change you can create is by allowing your light to shine through.

I'd been searching for my life's work for many years; done course after course, spent thousands of dollars. Yet the funny thing was when I heard the words: 'coach and write,' I realised I'd been doing it all my life in some form or another. As a therapist, as a listener, in my journals. It was something I just did, yet I didn't see it as something I could do as 'work'. Sometimes the truth is right before your very eyes but you can't see it when you're looking outside for it. Why hadn't I seen this before? I became really curious and this is what I discovered.

Somewhere along the way I'd come to believe that my work had to involve some sort of struggle. That I had to work hard for what I wanted, fight to get it. So the things that came naturally I disregarded because they were too easy. I thought my purpose involved some sort of sacrifice. I knew I wanted to be of service, I'd always known that, however I didn't connect it to doing the things that came naturally. I believe that was deeply linked to the thought patterns I'd built up around not being enough. I thought I had to prove myself to everyone and I was so busy trying to do that, I lost touch with what really lit me up and made my heart sing.

Much is written about purpose these days. There are adverts that read, 'find your purpose!' I don't believe our purpose is ever lost, I think we just go on a little detour sometimes. Or a big detour as the case may be. But it's always there inside us.

I've also come to understand that purpose isn't the huge important life mission I thought it would be. Rather it's simply living from a place of question and inspiration and acting upon its energy in every moment. Sometimes it leads us to huge accomplishments, but the focus is not on the end goal, it's on the joy that's experienced along the way.

Purpose is completely unique to an individual's reality. One person may be completely fulfilled working at a library, whereas another may hate that role. There is no right or wrong, just what is right for oneself.

I know a big stumbling block for me was searching outside myself for the answers. I listened to what other people said I should do. I listened to people I perceived were more knowledgeable than me when they told me my ideas wouldn't work. I thought they knew better. Yet now I see they couldn't possibly have known better as they didn't know what path I was meant to follow. How could they? Even I didn't know. They only had their own perspective, and that is filtered through their thought systems that are only real to them.

So writing and coaching it is. I let myself really absorb this and get clarity on what that would look like. The writing was easy, journaling was going to evolve into books. The coaching took a bit longer. Once again I spent lots of time in nature simply being and asking. Then, it came to me clearly. I wanted to help women transition from fear-based thinking to love-based thinking. I wanted to provide a space for them in which they could come home within themselves and from there create their authentic life — a life of truth, abundance and joy in which they would shine as we're all meant to do.

I had no idea how I was going to start. Through the advice of one of my coaches I wrote on a piece of paper what my intention was for my coaching and writing. Then I read it and let it go. I chose to have absolutely no attachment to the outcome, to simply trust.

It wasn't always easy. There were times when I doubted, when I wondered if I was doing the right thing in trusting my inner guidance. My thinking, my beliefs were so new and so different from anything I was used to, I literally felt like a different person.

Yet the more I embraced the idea of coaching and writing the more I realised it was my truth and that I couldn't deviate from that path. The old me had been an illusion and a very painful one at that. Step by step I walked on new ground, explored a new reality and experienced an ever expanding consciousness.

Before long I began to see changes in my outer world. Literally from out of nowhere people turned up to help me on my journey. A network developed of like-minded people who supported and believed in me. Everything I needed to build my new business came to me. All I did was stay in alignment with my truth. I stayed in a space of peace, awareness and knowing. It was phenomenal. I woke each morning full of energy and joy. Inspired to be alive and radiating from the inside in a way I'd never done before. I still had a few low moments, but I was able to move through them quickly and not get caught up in them. I could see they were just periods of thought that didn't lead to happy feelings.

I wish I'd come to this understanding many years ago, however, I believe we all go through what we're meant to go through in order to reach our own truth. If my life had been different, if I hadn't known the depths of grief, pain and despair that I have known, perhaps I wouldn't be doing what I'm doing now.

I see so many people living lives that don't fulfil them. Lives in which they play small, put others first and let fear stand in their way. I believe every one of us has a highly individualised curriculum; a purpose that only we can fulfil. For some that might be being a prime minister, for others it might be being a happy chip-maker in a fish and chip shop. It really doesn't matter; none of us are better or worse than any other. We are all precious, talented, beautiful, amazing beings searching for the same thing, our inner self, the missing chapter we skipped somewhere along the way.

By focussing on the outside world we forget that it's actually an inside job. It's so easy to believe we are victims of our circumstance. Nothing could be further from the truth. Once I realised that I was the creator of my experiences through my thoughts and choices I came to understand that my circumstances have no power over me at all. I'm free to choose how I respond. Circumstances are neither 'good' nor 'bad' until we choose to think of them as such.

Looking back over my past from this perspective presents a very different landscape to that which I experienced before. The people and circumstances I held responsible for my pain I now see as neutral. By neutral, I mean as having no power over me. It is what it is, and what it is has no meaning until thought is attached to it.

I found that from here I started to regain self confidence. I had always believed I lacked confidence. Yet when I really looked into it I reallsed I only lacked confidence in certain situations. Situations in which I thought I was less than others. Seeing it this way really freed me up to realise that I could choose to see that in those situations all that was happening was that I was thinking negative thoughts. It didn't necessarily mean that I could just change the thoughts and be different; the patterns were really ingrained. However, what it did mean was that I could see it for what it truly was and take action anyway, even though I didn't feel confident.

Fear was another feeling I was able to see differently. I'd always thought fear was a feeling I needed to take seriously. That it was telling me something such as, 'you're in danger.' Yet now I see that fear is just the product of insecure thought in the moment. I would think a thought, then feel the fear, and believe the fear was real. Most of the time I wasn't even aware of the thinking that happened before the feeling; it was subconscious.

I watched a video on YouTube recently called, *'The Dragon Story'* by life coach Michael Neill, and it really brought home to me the truth around fear. The video showed how people often go through life afraid of something outside of themselves, symbolised in this video as the dragon. In order to protect themselves from the dragon they constructed 'stuff' around them such as businesses, possessions, emotional boundaries, belief systems and so on. But the fear of the dragon is so strong that the walls have to be built higher and higher. Then one day the people realise that there is no dragon and that there never was. All there was to fear were their own thoughts. And so the walls can come tumbling down.

It's not always easy to stay in this awareness. I'm human, and there are times when I fall back into thinking life happens to me. Yet the more I deepen my understanding and expand my awareness the easier it is to return to that space where I am the creator. And what a powerful and exciting space that is!

****

CHAPTER THIRTY-ONE
A **Deeper Remembering**

"I don't see faces. I feel souls."
Stephanie Bennett-Henry

I'm discovering that writing a book can be likened to listening to a piece of classical music. Sometimes it's Beethoven's 5th Symphony, sometimes it's Mozart's Requiem. This morning it's definitely Bach's Air on the G String. A single string, pulling me gently, coaxing me to explore, to remember and to admit the deepest part of me that I'd locked away.

I was developing my understanding around thought and seeing positive changes in my life, yet I knew there was still an aspect I was avoiding. I was reading through some of the earlier chapters of this book and the part about seeing and feeling things differently to other people stood out. I've always felt different, and try as I did to hide it, I can feel the stirring once more, and I know the time has come to embrace it and to love it. I believe the terms used to describe this ability are Empath and Clairscentient. I simply think of it as highly sensitive.

It's a frightening thing to feel another person's pain as if it were your own: to take their emotions into you and forget what's theirs and what's yours, to know things other people don't know, to see a child crying when they're being punished and have tears in your eyes because you can feel their silent plea for help.

I never knew how to handle this 'ability' and no one around me could tell me. I remember trying to talk about it with my parents but as a child I was trained to be seen and not heard. I feared being judged. I was so scared people would think I was a freak, a mad person. I had enough trouble with feeling like an outsider without letting people know this about me as well. So I kept it to myself. But the trouble was it caused me a lot of pain and I didn't understand what was going on.

I look back now and see how I was trying to juggle my own negative patterns as well as what I was picking up from situations around me. But I had no idea I was picking it up; I thought it was all mine.

Having had space and time alone to deepen my understanding of myself and my thought patterns, I can now distinguish between what is mine and what I'm picking up from others.

The hardest part for me has always been picking up children's feelings. Because I know what it's like to suffer in silence, I strongly relate to them. I see them being told off, being told they're naughty or disobedient and I just want to shout, 'no they're not! They're just tiny, little, pure souls crying out for love! Why can't you see that?' I can feel their pain through every cell of my body. Fortunately, now that I understand this better I can feel what's happening but not take it on board.

It's the same with animals. I can tune in to what they're experiencing at a very deep level. Doing Bowen therapy on horses was so amazing because I was able to truly help them. Yet it was also very hard, because some of them were unhappy in their homes and I had to leave them there.

Another aspect of this ability is to know immediately when someone is lying. Yes, it can be useful, but for me, it brought intense pain because some of the people who were lying were the people I loved the most. I always knew. I could tell even before they spoke that a lie was coming. The problem was, I didn't want to believe it. So I disregarded it and refused to believe my own awareness, and that was one of the most damaging things I've ever done to myself. It made me lose trust in my own awareness.

I won't make that mistake again. I know now that every one of us has an innate wisdom, a knowing and it's vital to trust it. If we can't trust ourselves who can we trust? I pretended to trust people I loved so I didn't hurt their feelings. Yet perhaps in doing that I actually hindered them? Perhaps, if I'd stood my ground and not doubted myself they would've had the chance to change. Hindsight is a wonderful thing!

When we honour and embrace all of who we are we find ourselves in a space where we're truly free. I now see my sensitivity as a beautiful part of who I am, rather than a part I wish I didn't have.

Six months ago I couldn't have comprehended being in the space I'm in now. It makes me realise how time is just an illusion too. It's said that one needs time to heal, time to change old patterns. I used to believe this but now I see that change can happen in an instant. As Sydney Banks wrote: 'we are only one thought away from happiness; one thought away from sadness.'

I am truly grateful for all the experiences that have brought me to where I am now. Sometimes I feel like a butterfly that has just emerged from its chrysalis. First, I have to get used to the feel of my wings, but that won't take long. Soon I will fly, I will fly high, I will fly free, and if I ever look back it will only be to say thank you.

****

CHAPTER THIRTY-TWO
The Three Steps are revealed

"Do not be satisfied with the stories that come before you; unfold your own myth."
Rumi

A few months after I had written my intention for my coaching practise on a piece of paper, I was sitting alone by the lake as usual. My thoughts wandered to my book and as I reflected upon the journey I'd taken I heard the words: 'three steps.' I explored further and it came to me that my journey had been a series of three distinct steps: self Inquiry, surrender, and coming home. A wonderful peace swept through me as I let this sink in. I knew these steps would be the pillars of my work as a coach.

Through surrender we allow that which no longer serves us to be released. We let go of the thought patterns we'd constructed and held firmly on to, and as such the process is a subtraction rather than an addition. There is no 'adding to' there is only 'letting go'. It's the 'adding to' that leads us away from home.

There was something else that emerged in that moment, and that was a knowing that I had, indeed, come home. I knew that at last I'd put my demons to rest, my past was forgiven and I was ready to embrace my present.

I remember walking down the road with my daughter in her pram not long after this revelation, and I saw an image in my mind of the frantic woman I'd been when I first arrived in Belfast. It brought it home to me just how far I'd come, and how I was literally a different person now.

To arrive at last at my inner home is to feel whole at last. To be at peace for me is an expanded state of being that needs nothing from the external world to fuel it. It's the full realisation that I am the creator of my life in each and every moment.

It's from this place of beingness that my true creativity exists. I'd read about it and tried so hard in the past to find it yet when I did, it was as though I was greeting an old friend. You know the kind of friend that you don't see for ages but when you meet it's as if you've never been apart? It had always been there. I had just been looking in the wrong direction.

This state of beingness is in all of us, it's where and who we are meant to be. We think that what keeps us from it is the external world but actually it's our own thoughts.

Something else I came to realise along my journey was this: it wasn't what I'd been through that had caused my ongoing pain, it was only the fact that I'd held onto it. I'd identified with it and made it part of who I thought I was. Often I've read in books quotes such as: 'I am not my past,' but deep inside, I still thought I was. I thought I was the sum total of all the pain and bad decisions I'd ever made; it'd never occurred to me that I could change that by making a different choice.

The freedom that I experienced when I finally got this was amazing! I could release all the guilt! Everything that had weighed me down forever! I felt lighter, much lighter. And, I felt free to create and step into the next chapter of my life without bringing the past in to block me.

I became aware of how we all get caught up in the stories we hold and repeat to ourselves. Self perpetuating patterns that we believe ourselves to be. But they're not who we are; not at all. We are free in each and every moment to create ourselves anew. By this I don't mean that we are new people every moment but rather that we can create from a place that is not tainted by any preconceived ideas such as, 'I failed in the past so I will fail again,' or 'I was told I couldn't do it so there's no point in trying.'

I guess what I'm saying is that we can live each moment from a place of love, rather than fear. Because that's what it all comes down to in the end, love and fear. Everything else is just a branch of one or other of those.

It takes courage to make an inner journey. It's not always pleasant and most of us avoid it, yet the rewards are worth every step.

Another truth I came to know in coming home is that there's nothing to work out. In the past I wasted so much time trying to work things out: why such and such was showing up in my life, what I needed to do, where I needed to go. It was absolutely exhausting and prevented me from truly being present and enjoying each and every moment.

It's a trap many of us fall into, and it comes from the ego's need to be in control. The truth is we're never, ever in control. I remember something my coach said and it was this: 'We don't know what our next thought will be, so how can we possibly control it?' Those words really struck a chord in me. How can we possibly know what's just around the corner?

Another coach said to me: 'The point of power is always in the present moment.' It took me up until now to truly understand what that meant, but I get it now. Now is all that exists.

I use this analogy often in my work, but when I look at young children I see that every moment to them is an infinite pool of possibility. If only we could remain in that space as adults what more could we create! I believe we can, it just takes practice. Children are happy not knowing what the next moment will bring, they allow themselves to experience the full spectrum of emotions that make up the human experience without judgement or attachment. They don't even know what judgements or attachments are.

I thought life was linear yet I see clearly now it's not. When we act on inspiration in the moment life begins to unfold beautifully. Life is not linear.

In letting go and acting on question and inspiration we allow our lives to unfold from a place of authenticity rather than a rigid pre-set plan. Everything will work out perfectly when we release the need to control.

There will always be times when we try to control, however, unless you are the Dalai Lama who lives in total presence and awareness, and this is not something many of us can do. But, the more we practice self inquiry without self judgement, the more we will access the place we may, one day, call home.

This brings me to one final topic, the question of synchronicity. Have you ever thought about someone then later on had a call from them or bumped into them on the street? Or thought: 'How do I move through this,' and then you saw a book in a store that answered your question perfectly? That is synchronicity, and synchronicity responds to internal inquiry and awareness.

It was the Swiss psychiatrist Carl Jung who first coined the term and defined it as 'meaningful coincidence.' His writings on the subject were first published in the 1950s and by the 1970s the concept had begun to filter into films and novels.

In 1993, James Redfield's book, *'The Celestine Prophecy'* was published. It's a story in which the main character journeys to Peru to find and understand a series of nine spiritual insights found in an ancient manuscript. The first insight looked at these very meaningful coincidences, or synchronicities.

The more we live from a place of authenticity and truth the more we open up and see synchronicities in our life. In letting go — in coming home — we find that it's all there. The steps are shown, all that is required is given, and step by step we can create our perfect world. There is a power way beyond our comprehension, all we have to do is trust it.

And so for me one journey ends, and another begins. I take the things I choose into my new life, and I release and thank those that no longer serve me. I feel so grateful for all I have learnt, and I step into the new with peace in my heart at last.

****

CHAPTER THIRTY-THREE
Parting Words

"In a world where you can be anything, be yourself."
Stacy Loves

From everything I've learnt through my inner journey, this is what I wish for you.

- Don't wait for permission to shine. I think some of us play small in life, and without necessarily being aware of it wait until someone else tells us we're good enough. Don't wait. Life is too short and the world needs you. If you wait for permission you may wait an entire lifetime, and that would be a waste.
- Stand in front of a mirror and say out loud: 'I am enough.' Say it so many times that you believe it. You don't need to do another course; you don't need to do what someone in authority says you should do. You need to be you. Please don't play small anymore.
- If you're not sure what your purpose is, ask. Spend time alone, allow your thoughts to quieten, and ask to remember. Because you already know. Somewhere deep inside you, you know. You've always known. When you remember, do it. Even if you take baby steps to begin with, just do it. It will grow, and before you know it your life will be everything you ever imagined it could be.

- See the truth around guilt and shame. They exist only in your thinking and can be released in an instant.
- Feel the fear and take action anyway. Fear is nothing but a thought in your mind. The only power it has is that which you give it. Your true nature is pure love. Fear is just insecurity that knows nothing about your past or your future, it's just an illusion. I know only too well how difficult it can be to truly understand this, but if you can, your life will change forever.
- Don't do something because you feel you should. Do it because it makes your heart sing.
- Love everything about yourself. Never compare yourself to another. You are perfect as you are. Don't settle for anything less than your authentic life.
- This world needs people to step through fear and into love. We have all lived in fear for too long.
- And remember, when you step through the fear, when you take action from that place of love and authenticity, miracles happen. Miracles are just a shift in perception, that's all.
- Surround yourself with people that see your potential, that support you and acknowledge the greatest version of you. Don't waste a second with people who put you down or see you as less than you are. On the journey of life, we thrive when we're surrounded by our tribe.
- Be your own best friend, take your own hand, and dance the dance of life.

I leave you with one of my very favourite quotes:

'Our deepest fear is not that we are inadequate. Our deepest fear is that we are powerful beyond measure. It is our light, not our darkness that most frightens us. We ask ourselves, who am I to be brilliant, gorgeous, talented, fabulous? Actually, who are you not to be? You are a child of God. You're playing small does not serve the world. There is nothing enlightened about shrinking so that other people won't feel insecure around you. We are all meant to shine, as children do. We were born to make manifest the glory of God that is within us. It is not just in some of us; its in everyone. And as we let our own light shine, we unconsciously give other people permission to do the same. As we are liberated from our own fear, our presence automatically liberates others."

Marianne Williamson

The End

Acknowledgements and Thanks

As the author my name is on the cover, but there are others without whom this book would not have come into being.

I wish to express sincere gratitude and thanks to:

George Carroll and the members of the group 'Published authors in 126 Days – official Mastermind.' Your support and wealth of information saw me complete a lifelong dream! I highly recommend anyone with a book inside them to look up www.georgeiracarroll.com

Gabi Plumm of PlummProof. My amazing editor! Thank you for all your help in getting my book from rough first draft to where it is now. I have learnt so much working with you and it's been so much fun! Beware — more books will come your way. For anyone looking to have their work edited please go to www.facebook.com/plummproof/ Gabi and her partner Peter Marsh also make thought-provoking documentaries the details of which can be found at http://plummtreeproductions.com

Stephanie Hunn Ingraham for the beautiful cover. You took an idea and turned into the perfect representation of my story. Stephanie offers many fantastic design services please go to www.siyo.co

My coach Marina Pearson of www.marinapearson.com. When I told you I wanted to write you said to me 'why aren't you?' I have never looked back.

My coach Jenny Kennedy of www.healingjourney.co.nz for all you taught me about honouring myself.

About Belinda Bennetts

Belinda Bennetts' life changed when she discovered that the only person holding her back from realising her dreams was herself.

Through life-changing meetings, empowering books and a desire to remove the blockages of the past Belinda emerged as a passionate author and inspirational coach whose mission is to help others overcome their self-constructed limitations. She **empowers people to transform self limiting beliefs and blocks into fresh, powerful and focused mindsets that enable them to live with confidence, inspiration and authenticity.**

A qualified Equine and Human Bowen therapist Belinda now concentrates on steering people through their journeys from fear to love through her writings and coaching.

She is passionate about helping people suffering from stress, depression and anxiety disorders.

Belinda has a beautiful 3-year-old-daughter and a wonderful supportive family near where she lives in Ireland. This is her first published book but she has written many articles for a variety of different publications.

She loves to travel, explore nature and laugh with friends.

To connect further with her please visit
www.belindabennetts.co.uk

Or find her on Facebook
https://www.facebook.com/belinda.lawson.75

Printed in Great Britain
by Amazon